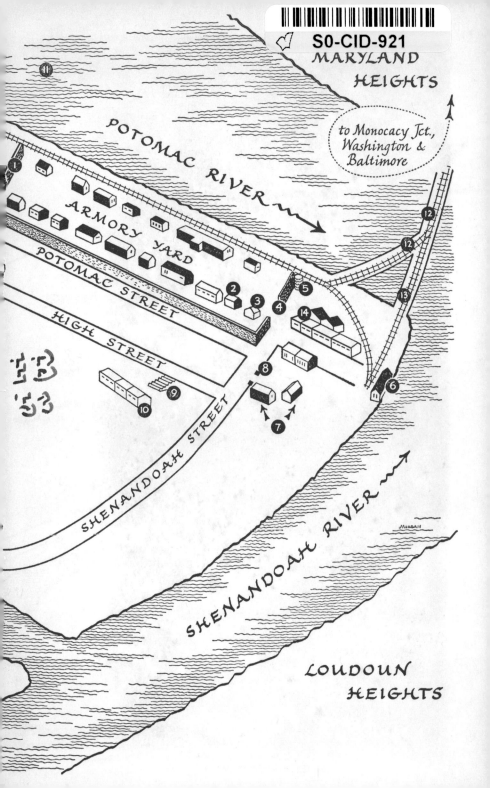

THE RAID

BY LAURENCE GREENE

America Goes to Press: *The News of Yesterday*

The Era of Wonderful Nonsense: *A Casebook of the Twenties*

The Filibuster: *The Career of William Walker*

O'Mara: *A Novel*

LAURENCE GREENE

the raid

A BIOGRAPHY OF HARPERS FERRY

Henry Holt and Company, New York

"The passage of Patowmac through the Blue Ridge is perhaps one of the most stupendous scenes in nature. You stand on a very high point of land. On your right comes up the Shenandoah, having ranged along the foot of the mountain a hundred miles to seek a vent. On your left approaches the Patowmac in quest of a passage also. In the moment of their junction they rush together against the mountain, rend it asunder and pass off to the sea. The first glance of this scene hurries our senses into the opinion that this earth has been created in time, that the mountains were formed first, that the rivers began to flow afterwards, that in this place particularly they have been so dammed up by the Blue Ridge of mountains as to have formed an ocean which filled the whole valley; that, continuing to rise, they have at last broken over at this spot and have torn the mountain down from its summit to its base. The piles of rock on each hand, but particularly on the Shenandoah, the evident marks of their disruptions and avulsions from their beds by the most powerful agents in nature, corroborate the impression. But the distant finishing which nature has given the picture is of a very different character. It is a true contrast to the former. It is as placid and delightful as that is wild and tremendous. For the mountain being cloven asunder, she presents to your eye, through the cleft, a small catch of smooth blue horizon, at an infinite distance in that plain country, inviting you, as it were, from the riot and tumult roaring around to pass through the breach and participate in the calm below. Here the eye ultimately composes itself; and that way, too, the road happens actually to lead. You cross the Patowmac above the junction, pass along its side through the base of the mountain for three miles, the terrible precipice hanging in fragments over you, and within about 20 miles reach Frederictown and the fine country around that. This scene is worth a voyage across the Atlantic. Yet here, as in the neighborhood of the Natural Bridge, are people who have passed their lives within a dozen miles and have never been to see these monuments of a war between rivers and mountains, which must have shaken the earth itself to its center."

Thomas Jefferson
Notes on the State of Virginia

Some of the material in this book has appeared in *The Saturday Evening Post*, the *Christian Science Monitor*, and *True, the Magazine for Men*, to whose editors the author expresses his thanks.

CONTENTS

THE RAID

a prologue

IN THE FORM OF A FOREWORD

The literary world abounds in purists. There are those who will scream as the wounded seal at the precious notion that a village can be the subject of a biography; biography, they will say, is the history of a person's life because that's what Webster says it is, and hence it cannot be the history of an inanimate place.

To begin with, let me define this book and tell how it was conceived—bearing in mind the fact that Mr. Webster has already ruled it out as biography. What we have here is not history, in the true sense. Certain supposedly earth-shaking events have been given short

shrift or ignored altogether, and what my dustier readers will call trivia has been gone into at great length.
This seeming discrepancy is not because I do not have
reverence for dates and precise facts; in my newspaper
days I was taught to burn joss stick to them and I still
do. This is an accurate book where accuracy counts
—in its picture of people; virtually every line of dia-
logue, for instance, has been culled from a reliable
source. But the intent has not been to pin down a lot
of statistics, which would be challenged anyway, because there is no more dangerous ground to tread than
that of the Civil War period. To understand what we
are trying to do I must borrow from another writer,
John Steinbeck, who says in *The Pearl:*

"A town is a thing like a colonial animal. A town has
a nervous system and a head and shoulders and feet. A
town is a thing separate from all other towns, so that
there are no two towns alike. And a town has a whole
emotion . . ."

Now the emotion for our village can be compacted
into a single word: violence. It was in the making long
before there were men around to complicate it.
Through all its ages, Harpers Ferry has been the core
of unseemly tempers, more of them, inch for inch and
man for man, than have been visited upon any other
community I ever heard of, even in the town where
Job lived.

You do not sense the emotion of a village. You learn
it, or you absorb it. Pitiably this cannot happen often
any more, because the village in America is almost an
anachronism, except in the remoter parts of New England and the depths of the Ozarks and storied places

like that. Today's village is a punched-out nothing. There is a main street with Detroit's finest mocking the noble horse as they nuzzle the curbs. The store fronts are rubber-stamps: red and gold for the A. & P., green and yellow for J. C. Penney, neo-Madison Avenue for "Louise—Frocks." When it is dark these mediocrities do not go away, but are kept awake by the night shift, the ghastly colors generated in the ubiquity of neon-filled tubes. If you travel through a village you hit its outskirts doing sixty, catch a glimpse of a sign "SPEED LIMIT 25—ENFORCED," cut down to forty and in another minute are leaving the residential area's twin on its far perimeter. If you stop at all, it is to eat in a restaurant featuring the gravy of the Greeks, or to have the tank filled at a station where the obliging young man does everything but blow the Buick's nose. Within two miles, even if you often pass this way (unless, of course, you are a drummer), you will have blotted the town completely from your mind. Possibly, if there were a dogfight in the roadway or the convening volunteer firemen were having a parade, you will remember a little; otherwise, no.

The traveler can't do that to my village. No main highway passes through it. It has been a ghost for a long time now. Driving over Route 340 to the west, you cross the Potomac at Sandy Hook, about a mile downstream, travel a little in Virginia and cross the Shenandoah at Bolivar, a mile up. You neatly by-pass Harpers Ferry and know it only as a forlorn little huddle of buildings, distantly seen and clinging to the hillside like monkeys to their mothers.

This kind of a town wants no historian. It wants a

biographer. The historian is hemmed in by dates and
spellings and those other symbols that man, in his
bumbling toward the stars, uses to try and prove he
knows what he's doing. The historian would look
upon the Ferry for its physical present, and go allover
sociological about the effects upon nineteenth-century
culture from its passing. The biographer, on the other
hand, can be personal or discursive, respectful or irrev-
erent, as he chooses. He can use the depressing present
as a point from which to travel back in search of a
bright beginning and the reasons for later sorrow. He
can try to analyze and arrive at some sort of conclusion,
not about a place or a time, but about that whole emotion Steinbeck has noticed. And in the resurrection of
little people who made almost no track on the sands
of their time, the biographer in a very small way can
transport himself (and, he hopes, his readers) into
the clang of it, the smell, the essence. He can, if he is a
lucky fellow like me, get to be great friends with a
town he never knew, except in its physical aspects and
in the faint tracings on old books.

   To arrive at this satisfying state, naturally I first had
to meet today's town. We had, so to speak, passed each
other in the street, but it was not until 1947 that we
shook hands. The city of Washington in any given
August, as everyone knows, can be three degrees hot-
ter than hell on election night. That August was no
exception. For weeks the temperature and the humid-
ity played tables stakes with each other, no bid going
much below ninety. There came the week end when
flesh could endure no more, so I went to the station
and said, without thinking, "Harpers Ferry." I was on

the train before I remembered that one chance encounter I had had with the tall hills and the cool hub-
bub of a couple of rivers.

Midway in the week end, it occurred to me that a
shack somewhere in the vicinity might be a good idea.
I advertised in a paper improbably named the Charles
Town* *Spirit of Jefferson & Farmers' Advocate*. The
place I bought is on Loudoun Heights, barely out of
sight of the Ferry but in clear view of Bolivar. It had
been the Pipertown Schoolhouse, one big room, built
a century or so before, of native stone and superlative
craftsmanship.

I grew to know my neighbors first, and wrote a little
about them—"The People on My Mountain." They
are wonderful people. The White House lies only fifty
miles to the east, but they go their way as their grandfathers did. On my road, which twists like those
blocks-long dragons you see in Chinatown at New
Year's and has a score of hills to the mile, the houses
are all homemade. Most of them are of logs, a few of
frame, a very few of logs covered with that monstrous
stuff Sears, Roebuck sells and which looks as unlike
red brick as anything imaginable. The women have
babies as often as God lets them, and have them at
home, usually with only the local amateur midwives
around to lend a hand. The men wear "overhalls" and
dip snuff and squat on their haunches, just as country-
men do everywhere; but my mountain men work only
when the spirit of the season moves them. They have
a hog or two, they grow some vegetables, they worry

* This is the modern spelling. For consistency's sake, Charlestown
is used throughout.

not, for at this, the lower end of the Shenandoah Valley, are the beginnings of the great apple orchards and
come fall there is plenty of work to be had. Whole
families go, in their own phrase, "into the apples" and
come back at the end of a day of skilled picking with
$40 or $50 to their credit. This one seasonal activity
carries the load for the year. For the rest of the time,
they may ride into Washington and its suburbs to pick
up $1.50 an hour on construction work—but only until
the desire (a 1941 Ford to replace the present Model
A, say) or the need (another baby coming) has been
satisfied or met.

In getting to know these people, in writing their
letters and taking up matters with the draft board and
finding out why Russell, the postman, didn't have the
permanent appointment he deserved, I came a little
closer to the Ferry. Most of the people on my mountain descend from the original wood-choppers and
charcoal-burners who were brought into Lord Fairfax's timberland to fuel the forges of the Federal
Works. The names are largely Anglo-Saxon—Longer-
beam, Piper, Nick, Young, Jackson. Their fathers and
grandfathers logged the country out and the game, except for squirrel and rabbits, went away from there;
but they stayed and they remained happy. This happiness is one of the little anomalies about the Ferry:
from all the grief and woe we're going to see there
has come a great deal of simple acceptance.

I did not reach a point of intimacy with the Ferry
for a long time. But when it came, I grasped that
whole emotion. I began to live with it, not very con-

sciously, but nonetheless conscientiously. Presently it had seeped into me, so I *could* feel it.

Any editor will tell you that the one essential in all narrative is conflict. The story of the Ferry has it, in fullest measure. The town's assassination in its sleep by old John Brown is the inescapable highlight, of course, but that was really only one incident in a long, long series of them. And all angry.

Nature was busy at the Ferry long before man, with his own diabolical techniques for raising hell, came along. A million or so years ago, give or take an eon, the waters began it. They were stored up over what we know today as the Valley of the Shenandoah. Illimitable tons of them, tossing in a gigantic lake. The lake became so vast and its weight so ponderous that somewhere, at some time, a conclusion was reached. Something decided that these waters must be the irresistible force. In due course, the conclusion was proved. The first of a series of rapes occurred and through the rupture the waters of the lake made their escape, over a way rocky but turbulently passable, to the sea. And in their movement they destroyed a misconception, namely that mountains are the immovable object.

After the rivers had created themselves and married, men came along. Indians and George Washington and old John Brown. The Indians may be said to have placed a blaze meaning violence on a tree in the Ferry, Washington may be said to have confirmed it, and Brown, of course, gave it dreadful meaning when he came, a gentle demon, and murdered the place.

Much of this book, necessarily, has to do with the
October night when Brown dropped revolution on
the Ferry's doorstep, like a leprous foundling; but
again, I say I am not writing history. I have looked
into the lives of the little people for the story of
Brown; and the large aspects of his raid must make do
with those few essentials without which the unini-
tiated might be puzzled.

Now all the while the men were at their mischief
Nature, which had begun it all, did not forget she re-
mains boss when it comes to "disruptions and avulsions." Every twenty years or so the waters swelled the
rivers to bursting. The stores and houses trustingly
built on lowlands were inundated and gutted. Until
1936 the townsfolk persisted in trying to use Shenandoah Street, on the riverbank, as a business center.
Then the last great flood struck. It wrecked everything on the street. It swept away the highway bridges,
one over the Shenandoah into Virginia and another
over the Potomac into Maryland. And the engineers,
being good ones, decided not to build again where
they had lost so very many bridges. The Potomac
bridge was placed a mile downstream, the Shenandoah a mile up.

The Ferry today has about five hundred inhabitants,
many of whom work in nearby quarries or the railroad
yards at Brunswick, Maryland, a B. & O. division point
six miles away. Shenandoah Street is ghostly, lined
with onetime business buildings, now condemned and
staring at nothing with that blindness peculiar to
broken windows. Not too long ago there was a project
afoot to sell the stone and timbers from the town jail,

forsaken as it stood when the waters hit: the cell doors downstairs ajar, the justice's chamber above with its rolltop desk crumbling, the railing for separation of spectator from malefactor in a drunken lurch. High Street forms the stem of a T with Shenandoah, and toils up Camp Hill to pass through Bolivar and become Route 340 to the west. There is a general store which shares its roof with the state liquor authority. There is a post office, undistinguished except for the mailbox on the sidewalk, a thing of severe planes and angles, built by a nineteenth-century metalsmith and remindful of blotting sand and the 's' that looks like an 'f.' Around from the post office, just short of a stone marker which tells how Brown slew a freed Negro as his first victim in the bid to end slavery, is Corky's, a beer joint filled in equal portions with tremendous mountain men and the unearthly noises of their music from the juke box. Just a little while ago signs at either end of the town, reading "WATER SUPPLY UNSAFE" were removed.

Frowning down upon all this are the great Heights: Maryland, across the Potomac, Loudoun, across the Shenandoah in Virginia, and Bolivar, back of the town in West Virginia. From below comes the incessant squabbling of the rivers, for when it was marrying time the Shenandoah came to her union with the Potomac as furiously reluctant as Katherine in *The Taming of the Shrew*, and she still scolds loudly to prove her temper is unchanged.

All manner of people have visited Harpers Ferry, from Jefferson to Julian Street. The ones in between were curious to see where "John Brown's body lies a-mouldering in the grave," not that they could, for he is buried in the Adirondacks. Street was fascinated by "an entrancing old town; a drowsy place piled up beautifully, yet carelessly, upon terraced roads clinging to steep hills . . . where one can ramble, stopping now to delight in an old stone wall, now to see an old Negro clamber into his rickety wagon and start his skinny horse with the surprising words, 'Come hither' . . ."

But enough. Let us go down into "The Hole" and meet our village.

ONE

the hole

1

The first Indians to inhabit the Shenandoah Valley
vanished mysteriously, six or seven hundred years before the tribes we know came along. They were somewhat like the Mayans of Middle America. They had a
civilization, poor things, and left behind them a few
fragments of it: writing, burial mounds and the cere-
monials for their use, evidence of tribal law and some
of the other claptrap that separates man from the animal and gives him neuroses.

Where they came from, where they went, nobody
knows for sure. They constructed their villages behind
stout earthen walls. They had gigantic mounds: one

near Winchester was torn down to make a right-of-
way for a railroad, and after four hundred wagon-
loads of stone had been hauled away the mass was still
six feet high. They were giants; skeletons seven feet
tall, with thirty-six-inch thighbones, have been found
in the vicinity.

There is a gap here, even in whispered history.
When the first explorers blundered their way through
the wilderness they found Shawnees, Tuscaroras,
Cherokees, Powhatans, and Iroquois—but there were
precious few of those. They lived as myths among the
trees and looked blank when they were asked about
their predecessor tribe. They were not at all warlike,
leaving that to such visiting firemen as the Delawares
and the Catawbas, and made considerable pests of
themselves to the wives of the homesteaders, who did
not like savage Indians but cared less for those who
cringed, and so gave them bread seasoned with contempt.

Whenever an Indian of the later tribes could find a
hearer, preferably with a little whiskey, he told tales
of the great who had gone before him. A few of these
legends survive. Most are mediocre anecdotes; the best
have to do with the Catawbas and the Delawares, who
did not belong around here in the first place but found
the locale encouraging to the blood-letting spirit.

The main trail, north to south, crossed the Potomac
at a point a few miles upstream from Harpers Ferry,
later known as Packing Horse Ford. The Catawbas,
up from North Carolina, and the Delawares, down
from the Susquehanna, had an economy-sized dislike
for each other—why, nobody can say for sure. Thomas

Jefferson took a stab at it, surmising that war must be the natural state of man or else these two peoples, with no conflict of culture or commerce, would not have traveled six hundred miles to have at each other. In any case, they met and fought, and in time decided that the few acres at the point where the rivers met made a fine battleground.

Theirs was war in the full pioneer tradition. Once a terrific battle saw all but one Delaware slain, all but one Catawba with a scalp for his belt. The Delaware, a moccasined messenger from a new Thermopylae, swam the river and started home; the Catawbas headed south, but as they jogged along he who had not won his scalp was twitted as a poor wight. Stung, this fumbler dropped out of the party and started after the surviving Delaware. He nailed him, almost on the banks of the Susquehanna, and when he rejoined his party the red in his trophy was still damp.

Again, the Carolinians made off with a captive maiden. She must have had much, that maiden, for they tolerated her over several days' march, binding her with vines at night with braves to sleep on the ends so she might not escape. But she could not move along quite fast enough, for all her comeliness, and she was allowed to straggle. A warrior slipped back and split her skull with a tomahawk. That night at the encampment the elders conferred worriedly. The maiden was dead, that they knew. But there were certain hazards which had to be given consideration. The same brave who had done for her was sent back; and when he returned all slept serenely, for he brought with him the soles stripped from her feet so as to make it impossible for her spirit to take the trail. The people around the Ferry still believe the tales about such souvenirs of uncouth aborigines.

Sweringen's Spring and Painted Rock are both over near Shepherdstown. The spring pulses rhythmically, and this is due, the Indians said, to the fact that a great Delaware chief was buried alive there and his heart still pumps. The crimson of Painted Rock, lovely in the autumn sunset, comes from the blood of heroes splashed against it in a days-long battle.

For all the quaint yarns they left, the Indians were still no more than a nuisance by the time settlement was well along in the Valley. The brighter ones learned to wait until the man of the place was off making a thicket into a tillable field and then irritate the housewife until they were fed. Others insisted upon attending religious services attired only in their breechclouts. A contemporary Comstock, who probably would have adored Gypsy Rose Lee, cried out at this, "Such heathenish attire—which is sinfully worse than lack of attire—distracts the young ladies from their devotions and turns their thoughts into paths too fleshly for the female young."

Because the valley was an oasis of peace in the years when the frontier ran red with blood, it could not hold such men as Sam Houston, who made Texas, or Daniel Boone, who opened Kentucky, or John Sevier, whose state of Franklin later became Tennessee. They and others went on west, believing the memories of the grandfathers but sure that what they told by the fireside would not come again.

The grandfathers claimed there had been a time

when the red man was a menace. They recalled how "Smoky Summer," that time after the first mock autumn when implacable winter is held off for yet another brief space, at last came to be called "Indian Summer"; not as we know it, a time to mourn for the dead June, but a time to be doubly wary, a time for the war parties to swoop down on men in the fields so foolish as to let the richness of harvest blind them to the danger of being alive. And because such things had been, in however small degree, the old hatreds did not die, nor the prejudices. A farmer came upon the traces of an Indian village in his new corn field. He halted his horse when the plow turned up the skull of a brave, grinning whitely from the rich dark loam. He went grimly to his cabin and returned with an ax. He pulverized the skull. At the tavern that night he answered a defender of reverence for the dead succinctly:

"They killed my father and my mother and my brothers and my sisters, in one raid. I have killed nineteen by myself and this one makes an even score.

"I will give no quarter to any damned Indian, not even a dead one!"

2

The Colonial Virginian of the Tidewater lived high off the hog, wearing silk breeches and powdering his wigs and practically never doing anything strenuous

because there were so many blacks to do it for him.
What lay beyond the Blue Ridge was called Land's
End, the name itself enough to make the Tidewater
planters highly indifferent to the place. Still farther
beyond, across what a poetic type called "the wall of
enchantment blocking off the West," or in geogra-
pher's language the Allegheny Mountains, lay true
nothing.

Divers casual explorers entered the region in the
seventeenth century, finding some ten thousand Indians in and about the Harpers Ferry-Cumberland-
Winchester triangle. The reds swapped off beaver,
otter, bear and other pelts for cloth, beads, knives,
hatchets and guns. (Similarly a little whiskey, but
since it served more to make the red man stupid than
to make him wild, there was not too much harm in
this.)

There were herds of elk and buffalo, fairly prolific
because bow-and-arrow hunting had not decimated
them the way men with firearms would. Bear, deer,
wolf and panther remained when the elk and buffalo
had been killed off. Pheasant, wild pigeons (mowed
down by hundreds in their roosts by lovers of pigeon
pie) and wild turkey fed the first white men. The
pigeons, in fact, came to be known as "hunters' bread,"
because their roasted breasts were mealy and would
last for the duration of a long march.

Then, in 1716, along came exploration in the grand
manner. Its sponsor and active leader was Governor
Alexander Spotswood. Spotswood was too damned ele-
gant for the New World, he thought, and took care of
his soul by being the number one boy in the Williams-

burg social life. He spent so much on his house it was
ever after called The Palace. He patronized the Colonies' first theater, where when the London troupers
were absent the local gentry put together dainty offer-
ings. He saw grow a culture ranging from the musicale
(with the summer nights resounding to harpsichord,
pianoforte, guitar, and flute), through dancing, fid-
dling, horse racing, and cockfighting, to wrestling and
pursuing the greased pig.

He was nonetheless governor of this so-called Colony and suddenly responsibility seems to have stunned
him into awareness that there was a lot more of it.
He was a flamboyant type anyway, but the expedition
he put together to go into the wilds and have a look at
what inscrutable Providence had given George I can
be compared to nothing so well as to a Hollywood cos-
tume picture in Technicolor, done by the current
reigning genius. A party of fifty was formed. The gentlemen wore green velvet, with boots of Russian
leather and fine plumes in their hats. The supplies
leaned heavily on the alcoholic: white and red wine,
brandy, two kinds of rum, champagne, cherry punch,
cider and stout. Indians acted as guides and two companies of rangers as protection.

Ensign John Fontaine apparently was mindful of
the generations to come, for he kept a diary. He told
how the expedition set out from the Rapidan late in
August. The first day they ambled along from one in
the afternoon until five, when they supped, quaffed of
a fine punch, enjoyed roaring fires and slept miserably
on the kind of bed their gentle bodies had not known.
The next day's trek was more leisurely; the party was

on the trail for only ninety minutes, covering a mile and a half. By September 5, with their fine raiment dusty and torn, the men scaled the first of the great hills between the ocean and the West and saw the Shenandoah Valley beneath them.

His Excellency did the occasion noble. He halted the expedition and broke out the booze, to drink toasts to His Majesty and the Royal Family. Then he cried, "Forward!" and they went on again, into fields as lush as any they had ever seen. They crossed the Shenandoah, which happily escaped Spotswood's intention to call it the Euphrates, buried a document claiming everything for George I, and then celebrated. Hear Ensign Fontaine on the incident:

> We had a good dinner [bear, deer, and turkey] and after it we got the men together and loaded all the arms; and we drank the King's health in champagne and fired a volley; and the Princess in Burgundy and fired a volley; and all the rest of the Royal Family in claret, and fired a volley. Then we drank the Governor's health and fired a volley.

Spotswood led his crusaders back to the more comfortable Tidewater, where he wrote a report about "Land's End," in which he oddly stated that "from the western side of one of the small mountains I saw that the Lake [Erie] was very visible." He ordered a trading post established, to give the French a little pause for thought, and then had struck some golden pins in the form of horseshoes and engraved "Sic Juvat Transcendere Montes" for his gentlemen, who thereafter considered themselves Knights of the Golden Horseshoe.

It was gallant enough, that expedition, but like most of the creations of the privileged it was not very practicable. Having claimed the territory, the governor did nothing to settle it. A more rugged type, best personified in the Pennsylvania Dutch, had that to do.

3

In 1731, Hans Jost Heydt, a German of some substance and by common local consent a fugitive baron, bought from one John Van Meter, a trader, ten thousand acres in the Shenandoah Valley. Using the Anglicized version of his name, Joist Hite, the might-have-been baron led sixteen families and a few hangers-on through The Hole and to a point about five miles southeast of Winchester. There, in collaboration with a Quaker, he increased his holdings to some hundred thousand acres and set about striving for the nearest possible equivalent to the civilization of his native Germany. The grant from Charles II allowed a tract to every man with a family, but Hite entered claim for every man, woman, and child, which totaled up to a vast deal more than His Majesty had intended.

Joist is of interest to Harpers Ferry for three reasons. One: The people he led, and the people all about, lived in the same fashion, making worthy of recording a few of the things they did, a few of the legends they

perpetuated, a little of their so-called culture. Two:
He went up against the august Lord Fairfax and
whupped him. And three: Among the hangers-on was
Peter Stephens, a worthless fellow, who shortly found
the crudities of the frontier more than he could bear.
Or perhaps it was not alone his sensitiveness that
caused him to quit the Joist settlement. There were
rough punishments in those days and Stephens could
have drawn "Moses' Law" for grand larceny, forty
stripes less one; "Wearing the Flag" for petty larceny,
thirteen stripes; or "the hating-out," a grim Coventry
that made a man utterly an outcast for lapses in morals.
Whatever his reason, Peter Stephens pulled out,
started back north, paused at The Hole, possibly to
suck meditatively at his jug, and decided he was tired.
His companion was a frontier loafer, part Indian and
all drunk, who was named, aptly enough, "Gutterman
Tom." They squatted, built a cabin and a boat,
planted a little corn. It is incredible at this distance to
believe, but the scant evidence seems to indicate that
even in a wilderness Stephens and his gutterman
were able to raise considerable hell; it is known that
Lord Fairfax tried several times to evict them, with no
success whatsoever.

But as they lived remote, the rest of the frontier
went forward communally. Except for a very few occasions in the year, the life was as dreadful as life can
become. Childbearing taxed the limit of nature's in-
dulgence for the women. Housework was com-
pounded by cloth-weaving, meal-grinding, soap-
making, and the rest of that self-sufficient routine

with which we are all now, thanks to M-G-M, familiar. In the evenings there was nothing to do but go to bed; nobody had any books, beyond the ponderous family Bibles, and tallow was too precious to spare even for their reading. The big occasions were weddings, funerals, and the construction of houses for newlyweds or new settlers. Of the three, the most titillating then (as now) were the weddings.

There was a procession, first. Fun-loving neighbors sometimes laid an ambush and tried to kidnap the bride. As the scene of the wedding feast was approached, two gallants were chosen to race for Black Betty, or the jug. The winner was triumphant beyond sane reason for his achievement, according to the contemporary historians, returning at the gallop to let the bride "kiss Black Betty's sweet lips" first. Then everybody took a slug and they went indoors, where the light repast of beef, pork, fowl, venison, bear, potatoes, corn pone, and whatnot awaited. When everyone had stuffed to a sufficiency and taken on enough of an edge from Black Betty's sweet lips, the girls convoyed the bride upstairs and undressed her, with much giggling and unmaidenly *double-entendre*. The men took care of the groom. Both sexes then participated in the "bedding down," a notable feature of which was a deal with a stocking. The girls took a rolled-up stocking, and each stood with her back to the bed, tossing it over her shoulder. The theory behind this primeval version of the bridal bouquet was that the girl who succeeded in hitting the bride on the head would be the next one in a nuptial couch.

Then the party went downstairs and began a night-long dance. Somewhere along about daybreak, a short ton of food, including such wedding-night delicacies as boiled pork and sour cabbage, was sent upstairs to the happy couple, accompanied, of course, by another Black Betty.

After the wedding, the serious business of living was immediately assumed by the newlyweds. The neighbors pitched in and in three days or so threw up the couple's cabin. The bride placed her dowry of pewter spoons and dishes, wooden bowls, trenchers, and noggins as suited her housewifely fancy. The bridegroom began his daily routine of twelve-hour days, sustained by a diet of mush in the morning, corn bread, salt pork, johnnycake and milk at noon, and hog-and-hominy at night, unquestionably being occasionally wistful about the table at the wedding feast. And, if the wedding night had not accomplished it, pregnancy was sought with a hardheaded singleness of purpose: big families prospered in the wilderness, small families did not.

In such a limited life, legends and storytellers had to flourish. Even today, on the mountain across the Shenandoah from Harpers Ferry called Loudoun Heights, those hill people I know are not far removed from the eighteenth century. They, too, make their own legends. They will tell you the dreadful tale of the man who fell into the rock crusher at the quarry, and exactly how his "laig was ground off up to yere." Three days later this victim will appear with a bandage around his strained ankle. Or: Legend—child blows off all fingers playing with dynamite cap; Fact

—Johnny Piper slightly burned holding firecracker too long.

The most imaginative and longest lived of all legends stems from a place about ten miles west, where occurred a phenomenon whose telling has been so vivid, over the years, that the Catholic Church has given it sufficient credence to hold an annual Mass in a field where a wizard did his dirtiest, and still was sent back to his limbo by an Irish priest.

What are known as "The Priest's Field" and "The Stranger's Grave" are on the outskirts of a village which is name-poor. It is barely bigger than a crossroads but it is known as Middleway (because it is midway between Harpers Ferry, Winchester and Martinsburg), as Smithfield, in one of those family aggrandizements beloved of Virginians, and as Wizard Clip. There is no house now, but at the beginning of the nineteenth century the land held the homestead of a prosperous farmer named Adam Livingstone, whose wife, to say the very least, was a woman of strong will. Livingstone was described as mild, genial, and ever so pleased that he had moved to Virginia, because there he has prospered. Mrs. Livingstone was a shrew, not to mince words about it, and was generally conceded to wear the Livingstone pants at all times, even in bed.

The Livingstone manor was squarely on the one great trade route to southwest Virginia, Kentucky and Tennessee, a pike crowded throughout the day with travelers of all sorts, from the Yankee peddler with his sack of notions to the six- and eight-horse-team freighters with their gambling, drinking,

brawling crews. And so it was not strange that one
night a wayfarer knocked on the Livingstone door and
asked for lodging.

Nobody knows his name; perhaps nobody knew it
then. The stranger paid for his lodging in the fashion,
by sitting up late telling the Livingstones what went
on in the great and exciting world. He was then shown
to his bed.

Hours later Livingstone was awakened by groans
from the guest chamber. He knocked and asked if he
might help. The stranger replied that he was dying
and pleaded for the presence of a priest. Livingstone
was halfway into the pants he had no right to wear
when his nightcapped wife, her arms modestly crossed
above the bosom of a flannel nightgown which was
modesty itself, declared her weight. There was no
priest closer than Maryland, a benighted state which
tolerated—nay, encouraged—that Papish religion.
(Only a few years before Catholics in Virginia could
not testify unless they took oath denying transubstan-
tiation and renouncing the Pope.) And even if there
were a priest next door, and Livingstone were fool
enough to fetch him, she, Mrs. Livingstone would
still bar her doors to everything Romish. Livingstone,
every inch the Milquetoast, acceded and went back to
bed. In the morning, of course, the stranger lay dead.

Since nobody knew who he was, he was given a
commonplace on the frontier—what ceremonial
could be improvised and an unmarked grave on the
property. In the evening the Livingstones sat about
the fire, discussing the dolorous fate of the stranger.
Suddenly the brands began to dance. They danced

right out onto the floor and for the balance of the night Livingstone did nothing but burn his fingers throwing logs back into the fireplace, only to have them dance out into the room again.

Livingstone, sadly shaken, went for a walk at daybreak. He encountered a teamster, who gave him unshirted hell for having placed a rope barrier across the high road. Livingstone could see trees in the proper positions but no rope stretched between. He humored the teamster, however, assuming him to be drunk, and went through the motions of cutting an imaginary rope. The teamster insisted the rope was still there; Livingstone insisted he cut it himself; the teamster tried without avail but was at last persuaded to drive through. His horses met no resistance, nor did those of a wagon traveling in the opposite direction, whose driver also said he could see a rope. This business went on for weeks, and Livingstone spent his days in a misery of being cursed for a barricade he had not erected and, moreover, could not see.

Meantime, on the farm proper, horses galloped when securely locked in stalls, until the barn burned down; the brands danced nightly; milk left to stand for a moment soured and the chimney periodically declined to draw, filling the house with smoke.

But the wizard, as it developed, was merely warming up in the bullpen with all this nonsense. When the sweat was running free and his arm felt right, he switched to his fast ball. The family heard a snipping, of the sort you hear behind when you are in a barber chair. And everywhere they went they found crescents cut from their clothings, their linens, their curtains, their everything from which crescents might be cut. The tale of these mysteries spread. Spectators came from miles around, as spectators will, the believers about equal in strength to the unbelievers. The men among the curious went home to find that the ghostly shears had snipped crescents in folded pocket hand-kerchiefs; the lady visitors disrobed to petticoats similarly vandalized. One such visitor, condoling with the family and denying that she could hear the snip-snip of the shears, quietly fainted when a flock of ducks crossed the yard before her eyes and were neatly decapitated, one by one, as they passed.

A brave German tailor offered to stay in the house and exorcise the spirit. He heard the snipping through the night and jeered at it, with a "Go for damn, you devil!" In the morning a fine broadcloth suit he had been delivering to a patron when courage overwhelmed him was unwrapped, to disclose the ubiquity and the monotony of the crescents.

And so it went. A party of disbelieving gallants came to give battle to the spirit and show their girls, who formed a distant gallery, how very courageous they were; the wizard contemptuously snipped out his crescents from the seats of their pants.

The record does not show how long this hanky-panky went on, but it was long enough to take pounds off Livingstone and make him gibber at the sight of a pair of scissors. One night he dreamed he stood at the foot of a hill, looking upward to a man in holy robes who was performing a religious rite. A voice whispered that this was the holy fellow who could drive the wizard from the Livingstone farm. Living-

stone went to his own minister, a Lutheran, who
visited the house but was so harassed by the wizard
and his damned crescent-cutters that he withdrew.
Livingstone took a more careful inventory of his
dreams, and remembered that the robes were priestly;
he turned then to a Father Cahill. Being a priest, the
good Father thought the whole business must be no
more than a practical joke on the part of the neighbors; but, being an Irishman, he half believed there
might be the possibility of an encounter with the
devil himself. So he spat upon his hands, hitched up
his pants, and walked about the farm. The wizard
paid him more dreadful heed than he had the Lutheran and fled before him; Livingstone, in gratitude,
deeded to the church the thirty-four acres now comprising "The Priest's Field."

Such stories are not uncommon on the frontier, but
in the area about Harpers Ferry, because of the pre-
dominantly Dutch and German antecedents of the
settlers, they lean most heavily on enchantment. A
secondary wizard, a man of flesh and bone, was John
Peacher, a Pennsylvania Dutchman whose powers
over thieves were incredible. Time after time, says
the legend, dawn would break to find a miserable
creature, black or white, sitting on the fence outside
Peacher's place. The shamefaced one would always
have a bundle. He would sometimes have difficulty
getting off the fence rail to state his business, and
invariably begged Peacher, "Please—unfasten me."
The bundle would contain loot, and the malefactor
would be inexorably bound to the Peacher acres until
it was returned to its owner. One of the better stories

of this great man, who would be a proud addition to
any police force, concerns the teamster who stole a
wagon's gearing from Peacher himself. The teamster
went east. But the farther he fled the slower went his
team, however he belabored them. His wagon was
barely moving when it reached the outskirts of
Georgetown, some sixty miles away.

Five days later the thief was back, afoot this time
and bent under the load of his pilferings. He mounted
the fence and sat there wordless, his booty resting on a
post beside him. Peacher let him sit for all of a mortal
morning, suggesting to his women that what they prepared for dinner be pungently, mouth-wateringly
odorous. When the penitential period had gone far
enough, Peacher invited the man to dine. But the
teamster could not get off the rail. He squirmed and
he reddened and he sweated, but he could as well have
been riveted for all the move he was able to make.
Peacher, at very long last, lifted his spell, forgave the
man, fed him a meal, and sent him back to Georgetown. The teamster made regular trips past Peacher's
place after that, but he never stopped again. And
from this incident grew the story that Peacher had a
wondrous wheel, by whose turning he could arrest a
thief in his tracks anywhere on the globe, and maybe
even beyond. In that country, then, "Peacher's
Wheel" became the sort of threat a city child recog-
nizes in the word policeman. "I'll take Peacher's
Wheel to you," spoken by a Pennsylvania Dutch
mama, had the impact upon her young of a cease-and-
desist order.

4

Some thirty years before the barbarians of the North
American wilderness decided that King George III
was obsolete as a tax-collector, there was a microcosmic
sort of revolution in Harpers Ferry. Its principals
were alike in that they wanted to make the New
World grow, unalike in that one had reverence for
European aristocracy and its perquisites and the other
felt no "furriner" had any rights to a land which he,
the pioneer, had hacked into productivity with his own
sinews and sweat.

Robert Harper, of course, was the man who believed in going by the old bylaws. Our friend Joist
Hite was the rugged individualist. And Thomas, Lord
Fairfax, was the plump and petulant symbol of that
which was dying, on this side of the Atlantic anyway.

Harpers Ferry, when it was still called The Hole
or Shenandoah Falls, was about in the upper center of
a gigantic area called the Northern Neck. This vast
acreage, of no value to anyone but Indians until the
Pennsylvania Dutch and the Scots-Irish from Ulster
moved in, has been known for the last couple of centuries as the Fairfax Grant, a misnomer since it was
originally ceded to Alexander, Lord Culpeper, by
King Charles II. The year of the grant was 1664.
Charles did not know fully what he was giving away
and Culpeper knew less what he was receiving;

neither appears to have considered the transaction of
much more importance than the passage of a cigar
from an alderman to a ward heeler.

Culpeper's daughter Catherine married the fifth
Lord Fairfax. They had a son, Thomas. When
Thomas was eighteen he received the Northern Neck
by entail. For more than a quarter of a century he
paid no attention to this real estate, having a sufficiency of the same in England. Then, in 1736, he decided to cross the ocean and see what was what in the
Colonies, specifically in Virginia.

He visited a cousin, William Fairfax, at Belvoir, a
plantation on the James River. Thomas was graciously surprised by the standard of living in the Tidewater, where his fine satins and velvets were not at all
out of place and where the body servants knew how to
powder a wig properly.

Before going into the fifty-year slugging match between Fairfax and Hite, it might be well to look about
for a comparison of the way the two peoples of the
time lived. To go fully into comparison would be
nonsensical; so let's settle for a look at two typical
houses.

In the Tidewater, the house had a curtain-raiser in
the form of a long drive, ending in a grove of huge
oaks, hickories and elms. The approach was circu-
lar, around a lawn big enough for polo. From the big
square porch the visitor entered into a hall with grace-
ful twin staircases curling upward. Dining room, library and parlor took care of the ground floor, with
the cooking (it smells so!) being done in outside
kitchens. The rooms were gigantic with high ceilings;

so were the bedrooms upstairs. Quite often the house was winged, with bedrooms on one side and a chapel on the other. Occupants: Gentlefolk. Politics: Tory.

But out in the Valley, your pioneer did with less. A gable roof covered a rectangular structure. The first floor was divided into kitchen and dining room. The second, little more than an attic, had little windows on each end and a sharply sloped ceiling. Sometimes there weren't even steep steps, but only a ladder on the wall. The fireplace sent out heat as well as hot food. It was flanked with cupboards. The beds were really shelves, the chairs, benches. Clothing was hung on the walls, not so much because there wouldn't have been room for a closet or two, but because such outward show was a sort of primitive Dun & Bradstreet's. Occupants: Workers. Politics: New World.

To get back to Fairfax. In due course, when novelty and gaiety had worn off, he realized there were a great many persons, many of them illiterate, living off the land a king had given his grandfather. This distressed him. He discussed the matter with another cousin, Bryan, and appointed that gentleman his agent-in-chief, with instructions to start collecting rent.

Now in later years Fairfax was to become noted for his charities. He was forever contributing to orphanages and such, and gave fine support to the back-country churches and schools. In cases of great individual need he reduced his modest rents (two to twenty shillings a year per hundred acres) to a token, a peppercorn annually or something equally symbolical.

Hence, it both shocked and angered him when the settlers, told to pay up or move, spoke harshly to the land agents and reached for their fowling pieces. It came to his ears that he was a considered a fiend of sorts, a parasite determined to grind down men and women he had never seen. He was confronted with the necessity for taking action, but before his slow-moving mind could suggest a course action was taken for him.

Joist Hite entered suit! A peasant, no less, dared to go to law with the lord of the manor. Hite called the one hundred thousand acres on which he had settled his followers a tract of eminent domain and de-nounced Fairfax for what we have come to call a racketeer. The suit dragged; the judiciary was as primitive as the wilderness itself, and courts sat when the judges had attended to other, more pressing af-fairs. Fairfax, in disgust, returned to England after waiting a couple of years, and took his grievance to Court. It was agreed by the King's Counselors that His Lordship had a case, but he was told, in effect, to bury his own dead. When Charles had given his grandfather most of a Colony (the Northern Neck covers some twenty-two modern counties in Virginia and West Virginia), said the royal savants, the respon-sibility for making it a paying proposition was solely and simply up to the holder.

Fairfax came back in 1748. The Virginia Assembly confirmed his claim against Joist Hite and dismissed the latter's suit. But the stubborn Dutchman would not quit; he entered a second suit, demanding legal titles to his land. Stripped of the whereases, his case had much validity. The original grant defined the property as "lying between the headwaters of the Potomac and the Rapahannock Rivers," when it was presumed the Potomac rose in the Blue Ridge. But when Fairfax learned the headwaters were far west, he sued for an extension and got it. Meanwhile, Governor Gooch had been granting titles to lands in the area theretofore believed to lie beyond Fairfax's boundaries. Hite's were among these.

The Hite suit lived a long time, about fifty years. Then the courts decided in his favor, but since both he and Fairfax were dead, and nobody by then was worrying too much about titles, the victory was a Pyrrhic one.

The manner in which Robert Harper handled his own land acquisition is in direct contrast to the Hite furor. As soon as he had bought out Stephens he went trotting to the head man for a title he could trust. And not so much to secure his purchase as to respond to hereditary law; he believed in property, in Lords, and in other things he had been taught to respect as a boy in Oxford. Nobody could ever say that his claim to the 125 acres comprising the best of the little spit of land between the Potomac and the Shenandoah was not honestly come by.

For all of which, Harper was a rather dull stick and figures in this chronicle only because he was the first man to build substantially in the village of violence.

the ferry

1

Two men met one March evening in the town of Frederick, Maryland, where Barbara Frietchie did not, as popularly supposed, make snoots at Stonewall Jackson. (Although Carl Sandburg says there *was* an old lady who wept as the Confederates retreated from Gettysburg and at last blurted, "God bless your dirty, tattered souls!") With one innocently acting the part of the mother, they conceived Harpers Ferry.

An unlikelier town-founder for 1747 than Robert Harper cannot be imagined. He was an arch-Tory, a native of Oxford, an architect, and a fellow who liked bathtubs. He should have stayed in Oxford, possibly, for he might have been a very solid citizen indeed; but then again, he would not have gone broke in Philadelphia, gone West to do a final job before proceeding to South Carolina, and seen a vista so magnificent he could not tear himself from it. That much of the poet was in Robert Harper: when he had once stood on Jefferson's Rock and looked at the hills and the rampaging rivers and the Maryland Heights cliff (somewhat later to have a huge ad for Mennen's Baby Powder painted on it), he was on the instant a resident.

2

We flash back to a bright October afternoon in Philadelphia. The city was booming and almost everybody who wasn't tied down to a job was taking the sun. But on the second-floor bedroom of Harper's house there was enough gloom to stock a pessimists' convention. He moved about, from cupboard to chest to trunk, packing his possessions for a move as yet without direction. Poor Harper, as he had been regarding himself for some weeks now, was a full-blown failure —and he was not yet forty-five years old.

He wondered as he worked how it had come about that one of the most promising careers he had ever encountered had blown up in his face. He could not lay it to lack of opportunity; his blood was good, his family substantial enough to have paid plenty for his architectural apprenticeship. Finally, he had talent; he had

proved it well before he and his brother Joseph joined
a company formed in their native Oxford to seek for-
tunes in America. But there it was.

For a time all had gone very well for Robert and
Joseph, with the one designing things and the other
acting as his business manager. Harper had vision and
had made quite a study of modernization and altera-
tion abroad. When he reached Philadelphia he found
this a commodity he could sell, for there were whole
blocks of houses which had been so jerry-built they
needed either fixing or a torch. His commissions were
sometimes more than he could handle, so that he had
to work like a comic-strip genius—draw in the main
characters and then let lesser men at the board letter
the balloons and do the other cleaning up. Moreover, he had also boned up on grist mills and this paid
off; the one he put up for Friend Burby was so fine
other mill builders clustered around it to steal its ideas.

Then everything seemed to go wrong at once. His
despair as he packed for his flight to seek a start in a
new city was too great, perhaps, to permit him to
take an honest look at himself. The ugly truth was
that he had collapsed of his own ambition, as do so
many men. He had not stuck to the old drawing
board, but had spread out into land-buying and general contracting. Came the day when some of his
creditors couldn't pay off, some titles he had not bothered to have searched proved faulty—and Robert Harper, Esq., was no longer in business. He was down to a
few hundred guineas, just enough to pick up his family and move somewhere—perhaps to Albany, in New
York, where things were said to be humming, or to

Charleston, where the great plantations were and a man who knew grist mills was a man in demand.

Business-wise, he was kaput, a blown firecracker, a gone goose, and a dead duck. He had completed his last job undertaken on his own, the church in Frankford he named for his native Oxford; it had cost him almost all he had, to do it honorably. He had given its sound deed to the congregation and called Philadelphia a day.

His wife opened the door quietly. He looked up from where he knelt before a small trunk with that wary expression all husbands learn to wear when they think they are about to be conned into something. Mrs. Harper had been Rachel Griffith, of a good Philadelphia family, and was an exemplary wife, but when this disaster came she put on so at Harper's mention of returning to England that he abandoned the idea. Even her acceptance of Charleston as a new home was incomplete; she had a female's morbid conviction that she would never again see anyone she loved here if they went so far away.

Now she surprised him and, as it turned out, most happily.

"There are some gentlemen here, Robert. One is Mr. Walker, the Quaker you came over with in 1735. They have some business to discuss."

Harper washed his hands and slipped on his coat and went downstairs. Long ago, as a boy in Oxford, someone wise had told him, "A Quaker's nod is no common bond," and through the years his dealings with the Society of Friends had proved the axiom's truth. He had built meetinghouses and mills for them.

They had bargained straightforwardly and when the price was made they had paid in cash, never voicing any but the most reasonable requests.

Walker introduced his two companions. "Friend Robert, this is Friend Steer from Loudoun County and Friend Fawcett, who lives near me on Apple Pie Ridge."

They murmured what men do in such instances. Harper and Walker spent a minute—but no more, for Quakers have little time for the trivial—recalling their voyage together on the *Morning Star* and chuckling over its discomforts. Then Walker became direct.

"We have heard since coming to Philadelphia for our annual meeting that thee plan to move. If thy will can be changed at this late hour, we have come to beg thee to reconsider and join us in Virginia. Thee can greatly help us there."

"But—Virginia? I know nothing of Virginia. And"—he gestured toward the ceiling—"I have been at my packing already. I could hardly make a change now."

"Thee will listen, though?"

Harper nodded. They sat. Walker resumed.

"We represent two communities. Some of us have made a fine settlement in the Valley of Virginia, near a river called the Opequon. Friend Steer's group is to the east of ours, in Loudoun County. We call our place Apple Pie Ridge because it is on a fine hillside and we have been able to grow some wonderful apples.

"We need a meetinghouse. We also need mills. If thee can come to help us we will see to a proper reward." He hurried on, as Harper hesitated. "Yester-

day we went to see the mill thee made for Friend
Burby. It runs very smoothly—and we have even more
power on the Opequon for the wheel."

"But when I have built your mills—what then? I am
not a young man, gentleman, and I must be settled."

Fawcett smiled gently. "I think thee would not wish
to leave our Valley, once in it. It is a lovely place. The
soil is rich. The climate is fine. And for one of thy talents, there is a bright future."

They talked for an hour or so, not haggling but
coming to an agreement as to the price and its payment in English money. Then they parted, with Harper promising to discuss the business with his wife
and brother and give them an answer in the morning.

"If ever there was happiness, it was in my house
that night," Harper wrote later. "We all made quite
a roomful and everyone was delighted with my change
in view, for my brother's and my wife's families were
almost broken down with grief at the fear of never
seeing us again if we went south. A residence on the
Opequon, they agreed, would not be going out of our
world and they were sure they would see us at least
once a year, when the Friends met in Philadelphia. My
wife, particularly, had great faith in a country inhab-
ited by such wealthy, quiet, and respectable people."

Next morning Harper and the Friends visited the
Burby mill. They watched it work and Harper explained some refinements he had learned about after
it was finished. By evening they had reached an agreement: Harper would remain in Philadelphia for the
winter and join them on the Opequon in April. He
spent the intervening months busily, interviewing

prospective workmen and going more deeply into new
gearings for mills, the relative values of overshot and
undershot wheels, and the like. He also studied maps
for possible dam sites near the two Quaker settlements.

On March 10, 1747, he mounted his horse in front
of his house. The street was crowded with friends and
relatives, the women very teary. After a moist and pro-
longed farewell, he rode off to meet a peddler and so
became parent to a town.

3

The whole affair was one of those which, viewed with
the smug and lofty perspective of a later time, seems
simply part of a pattern. We do not incline too much
to wonder how it is that the world is filled with so
many coincidences, even though editors say they make
bad fiction. The atheists might ponder this a little.
For just as the stars wheel their way on a known plan,
so do men wheel, except that there is no astronomer
who can predict man's pattern. In the case of Harper
and his new home, all things were at this moment fa-
vorable; at another time they might not have been.

For one thing, Stephens, who had come to be known
as Peter in The Hole, had aged and mellowed since he
first set up shop with Gutterman Tom. He took less
refuge in his jug. He had married the daughter of
one of the Hite colonists and she had borne him three
children. He conducted a sort of ferrying operation,

with a flat-bottomed boat, for people only. Animals had to cross a couple of miles up the Potomac, either at Packing Horse Ford or by the Shepherdstown ferry. Stephens spent as little time as he could at ferrying; he preferred to hunt and trap and did very well at both, bagging enough meat for his family and trading pelts of mink, weasel, wildcat and muskrat to the most reliable of his passengers, the itinerant peddlers. One of these, probably the most regular to pass through, was Peter Hoffman, from Baltimore.

But Stephens remained the individualist who had not been able to endure the truly frightful industry and thrift of the Pennsylvania Dutch, or Germans as they preferred to be called. He quarreled constantly with the rental agents of Lord Fairfax and sent back messages so insulting it is rather a wonder the Revolution didn't begin sooner than it did. He became something extra in His Lordship's cosmos, a "retainer" (as fatuous Fairfax continued to regard his wild, proud tenants) who was a pretty powerful personality and consequently obnoxious. Playing gadfly to the old misogynist at Greenway Court had some point besides the rent. It gave Stephens the husband's out: his wife was lonely for her people and wanted to move nearer Frederic-town (later Winchester), and if Stephens could make his fight with Fairfax look good enough he might move there without losing masculine face. There is nothing obscure here, for men are doing it this moment about jobs and new Packards and a variety of other things.

Now we have our pattern. An architect riding to recoup a failure. A peddler riding to sell beeswax and needles and thimbles and toys for the children. A settler who would rather be unsettled. And a heavenly spot for a man to live who, say, remembers the spires of Oxford.

4

Harper spent his sixth night at the best inn in Frederick. By then he was bone-weary and as filthy as a platoon of Turks. It had been a wet spring and he had contended with mud and detours through fields little better than bogs, and the exuberant wild life to be found in the mattresses of drovers' hotels. He was grateful for the inn at Frederick, for it was warm and clean and he even got a bath.

There were two of them for the shilling supper ("beef, mutton, fowl, vegetables, puddings, and your choice of beer, ale or porter"—oh, why do we have to grow up!). Hoffman was the other. He was a trencherman of big-league caliber, was Hoffman, and a German to boot, so little was said during the meal. Harper retired early to see what Nature could do about his aches and weariness. Hoffman remained below stairs, for he was the Associated Press of the time and he had a duty to the townsmen.

The architect was fathoms deep when Hoffman came clumping into the room at about midnight. He was a hulk as clumsy as his two pack horses and as faithful; when coincidence had had its way he became Harper's agent and remained with him for years. He was stimulated doubly—he had drunk a lot of beer and he had so well described the stock he carried, which he would display in the morning, that he was charged with the manic electricity that comes to all salesmen on the eve of a big deal. He wanted to talk and Harper, gentleman to the end, resigned himself to leaning on an elbow and participating.

They made an odd pair, in the flickering light of a single candle, the Oxonian with his clipped and handsome vocabulary, the immigrant peddler with his Weber & Fields accent and an imagination that could soar no higher than to contemplate a wagon of his own, "someday, berhaps."

Hoffman was no diplomat. He wanted to know Harper's business and he asked such searching questions there was no evading an answer. He was at once impressed. "You must be the great mill builder going to Apple Pie Ridge." Harper replied modestly that he did, indeed, build things, but deprecated any suggestion that he might be great (remember the land-buying, Robert, and the bad titles?). Hoffman was a traveled man and something of a celebrity wherever he went, but he did not often share a bed with a fine professional man. So to show that he, too, had vision he expanded on the beauty of the Valley and spoke warmly of his good friend, Peter in The Hole.

"Peter in The Hole?"

"Peter Stephens—that's what they call him. He has a ferry at Shenandoah Falls, where we're going."

"No," said Harper. "I'm going to Antietam Creek and cross there."

"Ach! Foolishment! You come with me by the nigh-cut and I'll show you the grandest place you ever did see, at the two rivers where they come together and make one under the cliffs."

Well, Harper thought as he drifted off into sleep again, it doesn't matter much. Eleven miles shorter this way, and I *am* in a hurry . . .

There was a frenetic hour in front of the inn the next morning, as Hoffman unpacked his merchandise and made what sales he could, giving the children penny trinkets to stimulate same. Then they started out, Harper on his good horse, Hoffman on his mediocre one leading the two even less distinguished animals with their packs.

"This Hole," the architect asked, "what is it like?"

"Wait till you see. Not only beautiful but one day it will be a great city. It has everything—much water power in the rivers, you can float the crops down from the Valley and carry them around the rapids and then float them down some more—all the way to Belhaven [Alexandria] or Georgetown." He paused and looked sharply at his companion. "I think you will like it. And I'll tell you a secret—Peter would like to sell. He wants to live again in the Valley where he went away a long time ago because—oh, I don't know. Trouble with somebody, I think, maybe Mr. Hite."

It was nearly dusk when they reached a point between Pinnacle Rock (misnamed, since it is not the highest point in the area, but so called in Lord Baltimore's grant) and "Shenandoah Falls." They waited,

the horses quietly grazing, watching Peter in The
Hole cast off and pick his way through the rocks in his
little boat. He brought one of his sons along to lead
the animals upriver to Packing Horse Ford.

It was a busy evening and one in which Harper had
to keep his ear awake. The two Peters talked excitedly
in German; Stephens was an Irishman, but he had lived
so long among Hite's people he spoke their language
better than he did his own. From the occasional
phrase Harper could pick out, Hoffman was throwing
a sales pitch to the end that if Stephens sold to this
great man, a metropolis would rise here before you
could say scat. "I began to think," says Harper's little
memoir, "that a famous mill builder all the way from
Philadelphia was something very much out of the common in these wilds."

They were hospitably fed and bedded. Harper had
a room to himself and he awakened at the first eastern streaks, dressed as eagerly as a child at Christmas
or a boy on the Fourth of July, and went forth to see
by daylight these wonders which could make the
phlegmatic Hoffman gush. He toiled up the first hill
he found, either following in the footprints of Thomas
Jefferson or leaving his own so that great man could
use them, and when he reached the top he stood for a
time struck dumb. Then, he says (and it's likely so,
because they seem to have talked this way) he ejacu-
lated, "O Thou Great Being above, Whose hands but
Thine could have created so much sublimity and grandeur?"

There being no answer, he wandered about on the
hilltop, looking at the view from every possible van-

tage point. Everywhere there were great rugged
heights, clothed in the best Nature could contrive. It
took only a grade-school imagination to envisage what
the summer might bring, and the autumn. He was
astonished there was so little known about this place;
he could not remember ever having heard of it. And
he decided, in this first look, to make it his home and
to die here. Scenery was not the sole inducement, of
course; you can always go to scenery. But the water
power was obvious and one day travelers and commerce would stream through this handy cut in quanti-
ties worth the exploiting. Here he could recoup.

He was recalled to breakfast and the present by a
tin horn. He found Hoffman busily trading with a
handful of folk who had ridden miles to be here;
Harper suspected the grapevine had announced him,
for he walked about in a lime-white spot. Some of the
settlers, doubtless briefed by Hoffman, urged that
he stay. He breakfasted and then went for another
walk in a different direction. When he returned in
mid-afternoon Hoffman was packed and waiting, eager to be on to his next marketplace. But Harper
begged off. He asked Stephens if he might not stay a
day or two and look further at The Hole. The peddler was pleased.

Negotiations opened at suppertime. Stephens had
only a "tomahawk title" to his 125 acres, but this did
not deter the architect. He said he would pay a fair
price and heard the figure sixty. Purely from the
human instinct which requires that a man try to
knock a few dollars from any price offered, Harper
said fifty.

"No. I am sick to death of this place and my wife's nagging to get back to the Valley. But if I don't get sixty guineas I'll leave my bones here."

"I think it's too much. You admit you have no title from the Lord Proprietor."

"Him!" said Stephens contemptuously. "Who is he to say he owns all this? Did he ever help the country grow? And another thing, he'd cheat the devil himself, if he was foolish enough to trade with him. If you buy, watch that nephew of his, Bryan, and that agent of his, Burden—they'd steal anything."

Harper paused another moment. Then: "Sixty guineas—done!"

A star-crossed village had been born.

5

The formalities of exchange were sufficiently quaint for Harper to write of them in some detail. They were conducted at the home of one of Stephens' neighbors, Esquire Hamilton. This gentle Scotsman had read of the soft-scented Virginia air while he could still smell the heather, and men being what they are, he decided he liked the imagined fragrance better than the real. He more or less stumbled on The Hole, and in one of its less prepossessing Aprils.

Hamilton was an elder brother of the Gavin Hamilton who was so great a friend to Bobby Burns, and

there is a dedication to Gavin somewhere which might
equally apply to his brother:

> As master, landlord, husband, father,
> He does not fail his part in either;
> That he's the poor man's friend in need;
> A gentleman in word and deed.

After a little unhappiness at the unceasing rains
("Does it always rain so?" Hamilton had asked Stephens that first day, and Peter had said, "No; sometimes it snows or hails.") Hamilton settled well and
for thirty years was magistrate of the district. His
home was three miles from the Ferry, and what happened on the morning of the transfer can come from
Harper himself:

After Esquire Hamilton had prepared the title bond,
I counted the purchase money on the table with the bond
in one hand and the other on the money. He requested us
to rise and addressed us as follows: "Peter Stephens, you
have sold your possession rights as herein described to
Robert Harper, a citizen of Philadelphia, and I now hand
you the purchase money. Robert Harper, as you have
complied with the terms as herein expressed, I hand you
the title bond, and charge Peter Stephens to put you in
full possession without further notice within one month
from March 18, 1747."
As soon as Esquire Hamilton had thrown off his official
dignity, I never met a more agreeable gentleman and he
welcomed me very handsomely and we were soon friends.
He from Scotland and I from England, we mutually
agreed to be social neighbors. Among other things, he
advised me go to Greenway Court Manor and enter a
patent under Lord Fairfax's grant from the Crown [which
he subsequently did].

For the moment, Harper took over the Stephens cabin and sent for his wife and brother. He made a deal with his Quaker backers whereby he gave them two days a week and devoted the other five to his own pursuits, one of which was construction of a highly successful mill. The ferry, such as it was, continued to operate, and a year almost to the day after Harper acquired it he carried as passenger one of the principal figures of the Harpers Ferry story—possibly even the villain of the piece, if you can be big about your historical evaluations.

He was only a boy when he and his slightly older companion stood on the Loudoun shore and called, "Halloo, the boat!"

His name was George Washington and he was on that celebrated surveying trip about which most schoolboys know.

6

George got the job because one of his half brothers had married a Fairfax, but he was a sharp young type even at sixteen and meant to get along on his own talents. It is a high pity that history tends to deify the heroes, because presently the world conceives them as somewhat more than human. Throughout his life George was human. There is no point in enumerating the human things he did—they are the same for all

men, and in youth George Washington was perhaps
just a little lustier than most.

Before we bring him fully on stage in connection
with Harpers Ferry, let's see what he did in these parts.
He surveyed for Fairfax, as will be described in his
own words. He carried in a neatly organized memory
a picture of the boiling rivers, to the end that an arsenal was established. He was fascinated with the pos-
sibilities of the Potomac as a mountains-to-sea water-
way, and tried with others to make it so, through the
Potomack Company, which had a more important suc-
cessor, the Chesapeake & Ohio Canal Company. At
fifty-six he ran Seneca Falls in a small boat, against all
advice and supported only by "two good men at the
sweeps" and a quantity of cherry bounce, which is
probably the liquor with the happiest name in the
lexicon. He hired and indorsed Charles Rumsey, the
steamboat man. And he often took the waters at Bath,
now Berkeley Springs, for those many ills to which he
was subject.

He'll be on and off stage from time to time; right
now he is cast as a sort of "Tennis, anyone?" type surveying his way through the wilderness.

He had set out from Greenway Court under James
Genn, with Fairfax's cousin George as contemporary
and apprentice. (Running the southern line, by the
way, was Peter Jefferson, father of Tom.) As has been
mentioned, George was a serious youth; his mother
was a widow and he had to make his own way. This
adventure was a big one and he kept a diary about it
entitled "Journey Over the Mountains."

George was a little sloppy in the grammar depart-

ment but that need concern neither his shade nor
us; his entries leave us an impression of youth two-
fold, in a country and in a boy. Even at sixteen he was
the farmer in his heart, for he rhapsodized about the
richness of the limestone soil.

We set out early with the intent to run a line around
the said Land, but being Taken in a Rain and it Increas-
ing very fast obliged us to return, it clearing about one
o'Clock and our time being too Precious to Loose we a
second time ventured out and Worked hard until Night,
and then retired to Pennington's. We got our Suppers
and was lighted into a Room, and I not being so good a
Woodsman as the rest of my Company striped myself
very orderly and went into the Bed, as they called it,
when to my Surprise I found it to be nothing but a little
Straw Matted together without Sheets or anything else
but only one thread Bear blanket with double its Weight
of Vermin such as Lice, Fleas, etc. I put on my Cloths and
Lay as my Companions. Had we not been very tired I
am sure we should not have slep'd much that night. I made
a Promise not to Sleep so from that time forward chusing
rather to sleep in the open Air before a fire as will appear
hereafter.

On the second night the party stopped at Frederic-
town where "our Baggage came up to us and we
cleaned ourselves (to get Rid of the Game we had
Catched the night before.)" The Indians looked on
curiously as these idiot whites peered through their
funny instruments, but George was as amused as they:
"We had some Liquor with us of which we gave them
Part it elevating their Spirits, putting them in the hu-
mor of Dauncing and we had a War Daunce. They
hopped and carried on in a most comical manner." He

had little more respect for the Pennsylvania Dutch in the settlements they passed, holding them to be "as Ignorant a Set of People as the Indians, with their Antick tricks. They would never speak English but when spoken to they all speak Dutch."

And then Washington's month as a surveyor was over and he went back, only to be called by Governor Dinwiddie in October, 1753, to carry an ultimatum to the French. Whether he passed through the Ferry at this point doesn't appear on the record. On this trip (on which the French, in effect, told the British Crown to drop dead retroactive) Washington stopped wherever there was a tribe. In addition to the note warning the French to stay west of the Ohio, he was a sort of a shill for the King, telling the Indians that England was their best friend. His brightest quote, perhaps, has to do with Aliquipa, who was no figure of romance as are all Indian princesses in the story books, but a woman "old and fat, as wrinkled as a frosted persimmon. Smoked a pipe and had a tomahawk in her belt. I do not think she would be a comfortable partner in the marriage state."

And he fought with Braddock and saw Braddock licked. And he fought for the Colonies and saw England licked.

And always, in the back of his mind, was the memory of the power potential in those churned-up waters along the two smooth river banks.

7

Nothing much happened in our village between Harper's arrival and the Revolution. There was no village, to be precise. A few houses sprouted up over the years, but the rivers were about the only source of news. The flood of 1747 was a great one, washing Harper's cabin away and driving him to higher ground. There was another in 1753, possibly the only one in all history with a poetic name—"The Pumpkin Flood." For days the rivers bobbed bright yellow, carrying away the crop stored by such thrifty Indian tribes as existed upstream.

The Big Town of the period was Shepherdstown, four miles up the Potomac from the Ferry. Even in Revolutionary days there were one thousand people in it, and in the early part of the following century it felt so well about itself a newspaper published what might today be written by a Chamber of Commerce secretary:

Shepherdstown is pleasantly situated on the southern banks of the Potomac River, some 62 miles from the delectable [sic] seat of the National Government and 175 miles from Richmond, the capital of Virginia. It contains the most intelligent and enlightened people in the Universe, as well as the prettiest and most accomplished ladies in Christendom. It supports mills and a manufacturing establishment, five churches, three free schools where the young idea is taught to shoot and two other educational institutions where the higher branches of learning are instilled in the youthful mind. It also supports two large and commodious hotels capable of accommodating innumerable persons, and the Baltimore & Ohio Railroad within five miles on one side and the Chesapeake & Ohio Canal on the other. But unfortunately, it does not possess the incalculable advantage of a Court House, a nucleus around which country people congregate and candidates for congressional and legislative honors "do most congregate." Therefore, being deprived of that important edifice, the Court House, we scarcely even are honored by a visit from the various candidates for office. We do not know why we are treated thus unless they think Shepherdstown is of little or no account and not worth the trouble of going to the little old place.

The editor who wrote this had every right to be rueful. When news of Lexington hit the hills, Shepherdstown was the rallying point for men who were to prove Washington's most reliable troops, sharpshooting woodsmen who could "hit the eyelash of a gnat without making him blink, live on an acorn a day, march faster and farther than anyone else and still have time for a dram and a dance." One of the most famous regiments was Captain Hugh Stephenson's "Beeline to Boston Boys." Each recruit brought his own rifle, shot pouch, powder horn, knapsack and clothing. All were required to be "men of character." They wore homespun hunting shirts with "Liberty or Death!" embroidered on the breasts, leather leggings, moccasins, and a bucktail on their hats. After a fantastic forced march they reached Cambridge, where the General himself rode out to greet them "and with tears of joy grasped every hand."

Of course, there were the Tories. Our friend Rob-

ert Harper was one of them. He had begun a fine stone
house and owned one thousand acres of land and a
ferry and mills. He was looked up to in the community. He was a born Tory who had brushed against
the pioneer spirit without having a bit of it soak into
him. Says a contemporary writer:

Mr. Harper believed it impossible for the Colonies to
contend successfully against the power of the Mother
Country. He felt sorely the effect of the rebellion, with
business daily falling off, no skilled labor to be had, all
social intercourse falling off and with England's feeling
being lost. Nothing that he could say satisfied the people
of the Valley and they all declared he was under the influence of Dunmore and Fairfax. However [and here
comes the usual switcheroo] this opposition did not last
long. The exactions and quarterly calls on him by the
Crown officers in Virginia for a heavy percentage of his
gold and silver, as a loan to the state in aid of the Royal
cause, soon cooled his ardor, and with a view to saving
as much as possible from the hands of the collectors, he
advised his wife to take, conceal and bury out of his sight
or beyond his knowledge and control, the larger portion
of all monies received in his businesses. This plan worked
very well, for several calls from the collector, although
the end was sad and anything but profitable. Mrs. Harper,
always active in business affairs (and much of the ferry
toll was paid to her), a prudent, conscientious woman,
while engaged at her housework ascended a ladder from
which she fell, so injuring her that she never spoke afterwards and died the next day.

For years this treasure was the object of "astrologers,
divining men, horoscope men, fortune tellers, *etc.*,"
the writer continues, but it never turned up. Or did it?
In 1872 a mysterious stranger appears in Shep-

herdstown. He says little and rides off every morning.
When he has gone it is said he took with him $60,000
—he had mentioned the sum to someone—which had
been buried under a large oak tree a mile or so outside
the town.

It doesn't matter much whether it was Harper's
money. If it was, the money's spent. If it wasn't, perhaps one day a boy will chase a rabbit and come to
where the rains have exposed whatever container Mrs.
Harper used.

8

Washington had a brief respite during which he became what he wanted to be—"a private citizen on the
banks of the Potomac." He farmed and he oversaw
and he staved off the idolators—and constantly, ab-
sorbed if not obsessed, he thought of his beloved river
and how it might be made the great avenue of commerce to the sea. In 1784 he was at Bath again, taking
the waters and looking over his holdings in the area,
when he met "Crazy" Rumsey.

James Rumsey was a man who couldn't keep a general store, couldn't run a boardinghouse, couldn't be
a miller. But he invented jet propulsion and he made
the first steamboat capable of moving against the
stream. Our George had a hand in all of this. First, he
examined a working model of Rumsey's boat, which
instead of screw or paddles used a water jet sent back-

ward through a trough, and was deeply impressed. He wrote a testimonial which, today, would be the stock salesman's dream:

> I have seen the model of Mr. Rumsey's Boats, constructed to work against stream; have examined the power upon which it acts;—have been an eye-witness to an actual experiment in running water of some rapidity; & do give it as my opinion (although I had little faith before) that he has discovered the Art of Propelling Boats by mechanism & small manual assistance against rapid currents;—that the discovery is of vast importance—may be of the greatest usefulness in our inland navigation—& if it succeeds, of which I have no doubt, that the value of it is greatly enhanced by the simplicity of the works, which when seen and explained to, might be executed by the commonest mechanics.

This was "given under his hand" and proved of some value to "Crazy" Rumsey, although it did not get him the backers he needed. He more or less had to forge his first boat with his own hands, using what funds he could earn himself. Some of the funds came from a primary Washington dream—the opening to navigation of the Potomac, all the way from the mountains to Tidewater.

When the Potomack Company was formed, to blast its way through the rocks at Great and Little Falls, Rumsey was hired to supervise. This was in 1785, a year in which George's journal recorded that he "dined at Harpers Ferry and Took a view of the River." Rumsey by-passed Great Falls without too much trouble and his canal was the wonder of its day —but in the fashion of the ball-point pen. Everybody talked about it, but then everybody began to point out

that commerce was to be made only by going a lot farther west than Georgetown and what was to be done
about that? Rumsey was moving upriver, blasting
as he went, but he was having his troubles. His la-
borers drank too much and knew too little about
blasting powder. When half a dozen of them went,
in sections, to Kingdom Come, Rumsey reported la-
conically, "The workmen use the powder Rather too
Extravagantly." After fourteen months at 200 pounds
a year, he quit the job to continue experimenting on
his boat.

Washington's testimonial won him exclusive rights
to navigate by steam on Virginia's inland waterways.
He set up shop at Shepherdstown and was a garrulous
fellow about his invention, for there he got the name
"Crazy." He worked through the summer of 1786 on
his boat, but ice blocked the river early that year. The
next spring he tried again, only to have the boiler
burst. The second boiler generated so much heat it
melted the solder holding together some of the other
parts. By the time Rumsey had devised a harder solder
it was December, and here came the ice, and there
went Rumsey's boat into the rocks.

Such disappointments were as regular as breakfast,
but there did come at last a December day in 1787
when a crowd assembled on the cliffs just west of the
Ferry. Among those invited by Rumsey were nota-
bles: General Gates, Captain Shephard, Major Bedinger and their ladies, and a few of the more courageous (including Mrs. Bedinger, who knitted on
something throughout) went aboard. Rumsey threw
his levers and his ungainly business moved out into

the river, placid at that point. General Gates had remained ashore and when the boat started upstream he jumped up and down like a kid at a circus parade, yelling, "She moves; by Gad! sirs, she moves!" For a couple of hours Rumsey navigated upstream and down, hitting a dizzy three miles an hour against the current. Then he took his bows and went off to Philadelphia to hunt for backers.

He found Benjamin Franklin interested and encouraging, and proceeded to London where the money was, with letters to Sir Benjamin Rush and James Watt, signed by Franklin as "president of the Rumsey society." Sir Benjamin was friendly enough, but Watt was on the chill side. After all, the man who as a boy had the wit to see that the force of steam could lift the lid of a kettle could hardly have been expected to give this colonial too much encouragement; the best he could do for Rumsey, he said, was help him provided he fired his American backers. This Rumsey declined to do, and went through a heartbreaking period of going it alone.

A patron went bankrupt. Rumsey finished a boat called the *Columbian Maid* by borrowing, and when the *Maid* went coy on him in a trial on the Thames he had to go underground awhile to escape debtors' prison. He went to Ireland and constructed a canal, came back prepared for a new trial, and had his boat attached just before he would have proved to the English she could sail. Then, only a week after his sudden death, his boat performed magnificently on the Thames.

They diagnosed the cause of his death as a cerebral

hemorrhage—but the blood in the brain comes from the heart, and the real story's probably there.

As an ironical postscript, one of the young men he met in London, strange to steam and there only to sell the British Navy a torpedo-boat invention, was Robert Fulton.

9

They've dragged the ubiquitous Washington away from Mount Vernon and made a president out of him. He's fought a war to make a republic and now he has to be President to make it stick. In Europe, mostly, because there this miracle of a new nation is not quite believed, and if believed is not quite liked because America is so rich, there are rumors and even threats of wars. And although few of these penetrate to the quiet remoteness of Harpers Ferry, it is about to enter another phase—let's call it puberty.

When the French began prancing around and indicating an intention any moment of busting the new United States in the nose, Timothy Pickering, Secretary of War, became alarmed. He urged Congress to make some provision for the manufacture and storage of arms. God knows we needed something like that. The arms with which the Revolution had been fought formed as weird a collection of antiques and improvisations as could be imagined.

With what money the Continental Congress could

scrape up, we had bought what we could get, from the Dutch, the French, the Germans. Most of it was junk; there were only two standard weapons in the Revolution—standard in the sense that they had been designed and manufactured abroad for the sole purpose of killing men. One was the French 1763, the other the British "Brown Bess," so named because a fancy-pants regiment under Elizabeth I was privileged to stain its muskets stocks and barrels brown. Otherwise, the Revolutionists used what they had, old muskets, squirrel rifles, everything except blowguns.

When Pickering sent his recommendation to the Third Congress, in 1794, the President endorsed it, and recommended federal armories and arsenals at Springfield, Massachusetts, and Harpers Ferry. The arsenal at Springfield, as well as that at Carlisle, Pennsylvania, were state, and they were acquired for federal use. Harpers Ferry started from the ground.

The 125-acre Harper tract was purchased, as were 310 acres from a man named Rutherford, on Bolivar Heights. Ultimately, the Harper tract held these buildings, reading from east to west: the arsenal, two buildings on Shenandoah Street, near that river; the engine house where Brown made his last stand; the paymaster's office; and then the several structures of the armory, all strung along the banks of the Potomac. Considering the time and the pennies in an infant nation's piggy bank, construction was swift; the land was acquired in June, 1796, and the first guns were produced toward the end of that year. They were copies of the 1763 French musket, and sorry copies, indeed.

Our Congress, then as now nipple-headed, had

limited the number of workmen in all federal arsenals to one hundred. It had authorized no funds for
proper tools or machinery. Consequently, everything
was handmade and it was not until John H. Hall came
along that there was any effort toward standardization.
The first muskets differed one from the other as do
fingerprints, so if a firelock went wrong the gun was
inoperative until another could be fabricated.

Washington's endorsement of the Harpers Ferry
site, sentimental as it was, could not be called unreal-
istic. "It is," he wrote the Congress, "the most eligible
spot on the river, in my opinion." And it was, except
for one factor nobody seems to have thought of at the
time: it was completely indefensible in time of war.
Lying as it did, in a bowl below three towering
heights, it could not be held by any number of defenders, unless they also held the hills. Stonewall
Jackson demonstrated this in '63, when he took the
garrison of twelve thousand after the briefest of artillery barrages and skirmishes.

Otherwise, the Ferry had what it took. There was
the so-often mentioned water power, capable of turning any number of wheels. On Loudoun Heights,
where some 1,400 acres were leased in perpetuity
from the Fairfax estate, was abundant timber for
the charcoal made by the ancestors of those people
I know. And there was plenty of iron with forges
to work it. The early iron works were ingenious
and efficient; the Bloomery, about a mile up the
Shenandoah at Big Eddy, was typical. The blast furnace was built against the hillside, with a roadway
above so it could be charged from wagons. The huge

bellows were water-powered. In front, on the lower
level, was the casting house. Some of the larger forges
had water-driven trip-hammers to beat out pigs for
a more refined iron the smith could work, and the
Bloomery was one of them.

10

If you care to be sociological about it, the time of tran-
sition in the life of a community can be highly in-
formative—and very, very dull. In the case of our village, it is good to say, there are so few records for that
period between the turn of the nineteenth century
and the coming of the railroad, that all we have to go
on is a fragment here and there. Which, as far as I am
concerned, is quite enough.

We have seen a village conceived and given a godfather in the person of Washington. We have watched
its infancy and seen it into puberty. It seems to have
had no boyhood, none anyone cared to record, at
least. There it was, a ferrying point on the highroad
to the West; and here it is, beginning to be a man with
factories rising, from which will belch smoke and the
portent of disaster.

The tradition of violence alone is consistent. It runs
through every period of Harpers Ferry's years. Even
so romantic and simple a thing as the rock on which
Jefferson sat to jot some of his *Notes on the State of
Virginia* had to be connected with conflict—while he

sat there, in an interim period, and when he became
President. Or maybe there is too much significance
being read into this sort of thing, which is a trap into
which all biographers fall.

The Rock. It was on the highest eminence overlooking the Shenandoah and may now be reached by
a flight of twenty-four steps, hewn from the solid rock
by the slaves who built Robert Harper's house, and
then by puffing up a steep path. There was a smaller
rock above, gingerly balanced so that it would move a
little if a child pushed hard enough. As Jefferson sat
upon it, and later carved his initials into its side, he
noticed a gigantic oak over on the Maryland shore,
with eagles swooping about it; the memory stayed
with him. When he became President, he wrote Superintendent Perkins of the new arsenal to send him
an eaglet. Perkins snared three. One went to the King
of Spain as a gift of state. The King sent back an
Andalusian ram, first of its breed in America. The
populace roared at the idea of accepting gifts from
foreign despots. Before the roar had hit anything like
a high note the ram, grazing on the White House
lawn, was tormented by a boy named Reed and butted
him dead. The roaring increased . . . and there, in
the most innocent of actions, was a notation in the
heavy book of violence.

And even before this, the Rock was not immune.
That noise the French were making, back there a
page or two, bothered officialdom to the extent of the
establishment (on the 301 acres bought from Mr.
Rutherford on Bolivar Heights) of an army post.
Camp Hill, they called it then. An officer, a Whig as

rabid as the Union Leaguers who used to glower toward the White House in the Roosevelt administration as though to blast by their hatred the souls of all New Dealers, became so infuriated at some Jefferson policy one day that he called out part of his company, marched up to Jefferson's Rock, and toppled it over the cliff, initials and all. A Jeffersonian officer challenged the Whig to a duel. The commanding officer discovered all this nonsense in time, tucked the two officers in separate parts of the guardhouse until they had cooled off, and ended the incident.

Except, of course, for such resurrections as this, when it is used to strike pitch note for a little town that was simply born to trouble.

The workers brought in to man the Works, as the arsenal-armory-rifle factory will be called hereafter, did their manly share. Naturally, the first merchants to follow the signing of contracts for construction of the Works were the dispensers of grog. Their best customers were a queer lot. There were the Germans, who preferred beer, and the fierily dour Scots-Irish, who were so mixed up with migration and persecution nothing but whiskey would help them. And whiskey made them bellicose. They were Ulstermen, mostly, descendants of the Scots who had fled from Cromwell. Because they were Presbyterians, Ulster took a turn at persecuting them, under William and Mary, Anne, and the Georges. So they came to Pennsylvania, and thence to Harpers Ferry and there, the idea of having to fight every step of the way having been so forcibly instilled, they took out their tempers on the Pennsylvania Dutch.

On German feast days, the Irish would hold a mock parade, with Saint Sheila in the lead, her apron filled with potatoes. On St. Patrick's Day the Germans carried his effigy through the streets, necklaced with sauerkraut. That, plus the grog, plus the beer, created what might euphemistically be called difference of opinion.

Withal, it was progressive. Churches and schools were built, the most spectacular of the former being St. Peter's, on the hill leading to the Rock, of which an early traveler wrote:

> If the "Gates of Hell" try to prevail against this institution, they had best assault from above. There will be no chance for attacking the foundation, though, for it is solid rock, extending no one knows how far into the bowels of the earth or through them, perhaps, all the way to the supposed location of those terrible gates themselves.

The turnpike to Middleway, or Wizard Clip, was constructed in the most modern way, by John Loudon McAdam's paving plan whereby large stones were laid as a base and smaller stones placed atop them until the crown itself could be hard-packed with gravel. To ride this miracle of smoothness cost only 2 cents a mile, horse and buggy; to make the one-day trip into Washington by stage cost $4.

In 1819 Herr's Island, up the Shenandoah a few blocks and later named Virginius, had a small boom of its own. The government employed John H. Hall, a Maine man, to make rifles there. His factory was added to a tannery, oil refinery, grist- and saw-mill, and it operated on what might be called the first mass-production basis for arms in history. Hall had patented the first breech-loading flintlock in 1811. His rifle could fire eight rounds a minute whereas the musket could fire only two. His subsidiary inventions, of machines to turn out small parts, made all guns one in their components, so if a trigger broke another could be fitted immediately. Among other things, Hall had a lacquer so tough it made metals impervious to water, acid, and oil; it could be removed only by abrasion. When the Works were destroyed in the Civil War, the formula vanished forever.

Oh, yes. One Fontaine Beckham advertised a couple of houses for rent on Herr's Island in 1830. Remember Fontaine. He will be a big man, for the fleeting part of a second, a little further along.

The signs of progress to be found in the Ferry until 1834 were, in all truth, tiny ones. That was the year the railroad came; that was the year which made it doubly inevitable that our village must die.

11

The year 1832, in Harpers Ferry, was not one of any particular moment. The Works were producing, the paymaster was a faithful soul, and, save for the Saturday night brawls between the Irish and the Pennsylvania Dutch, there was peace. But off to the east there was neither peace nor its harbinger, although no one in the Ferry ascribed any overwhelming significance to it. The future was too far away; it is

easy enough now to move back into 1832 and be
profound about what was to come, knowing it in the
tiniest detail, but our village had no Nostradamus to
give its people warning.

In the final analysis, what destroyed Harpers Ferry
was what had made it: its physical location. Its site
had been ideal for an armory and seemed to John
Brown equally ideal as the springboard from which
to plunge into his holy war. And there was no other
place for a railroad to be built, which made the Civil
War years tough ones indeed for the Ferrians.

●The pattern of dissension which makes the Ferry
unique among towns was adhered to most faithfully
by the destinies when it came time for a railroad to
punch its way through to the West. The Baltimore &
Ohio's directors were never content with the ohs and
ahs they got for running trains to Elliott's Mills and
then to Frederick. Their aim was a Main Stem reach-
ing all the way to the banks of the Ohio. To achieve
it, they had to go by way of Harpers Ferry, because
any other route would have been prohibitively costly.

G. Washington turns up here again, although he
has been dead for decades. His Potomack Company
had failed to open the river to navigation. It owned
certain franchises and assets which were of value,
however, and these were acquired by the Chesapeake
& Ohio Canal Company in 1828. The canal company
had plenty of power, in its brief day; it was boom time
for artificial waterways. "Clinton's Folly" had become
the Grand Canal, no less, and individuals and com-
monwealths were rushing to duplicate it in a variety
of places: from Rondout, on the Hudson, to Hones-

dale, Pennsylvania; the Morris & Essex across New
Jersey; from New Haven to Northampton, Massachusetts; from Lowell to Boston. Others were in the planning stage in Ohio, in the Delaware and Lehigh
Valleys, and wherever in New York connecting canals
could tie in with the eminently successful Erie.

The canal builders all looked to the Erie for inspi-
ration, meanwhile making jokes about the iron horse
not unlike the "Get a horse!" of a later time. In New
York great stretches of virtually uninhabited territory were populated almost overnight and along the
canal's banks new towns appeared, like miracles in
the puff of a magician's smoke. The barges moved
from the inland production centers to market in an
unbroken line, nose to tail; and the agricultural areas
and the cities knew profits the like of which they had
never dared to dream.

Thus, when the Baltimore & Ohio Railroad reached
Point of Rocks, about sixty miles west of the Camden
Street station, the canal people were already there.
Around towering Catoctin Mountain, on the Potomac's Maryland shore, there was a bare shelf of space,
hardly enough for a turnpike; twice again in the
dozen miles to Harpers Ferry the available bank space
narrowed down to the irreducible minimum for a
transportation artery. The B. & O. needed that shelf,
whose only other alternative for a route was a bridge
across the Shenandoah at Point of Rocks. But the canal
people, regarding railroaders as upstarts with a short-
lived gimcrack to promote, decided to fight.

The canal's lobbyists introduced some weird legislation at Annapolis, which would have forever banned

the building of any bridge over the canal, permitted
the importation of slaves from Virginia to do the dirty
work, and required the purchase of entire farms
whenever the canal passed over any one of their acres.
The last condition was the one that revealed the legislation for what it was—a determined effort to inhibit
the railroad from paralleling the canal at any feasible
distance—and because it was so venal it was defeated.
But the C. & O. Canal Company got an injunction
holding the railroad at Point of Rocks, on the ground
it had prior right to any right-of-way west to the
Ferry, and after a bitter fight made it stick in a Court
of Appeals decision.

The B. & O. then tried to make a deal, agreeing to
pick up the whole $14,000 tab for joint construction
on the three stretches between Harpers Ferry and
Point of Rocks, but the canal company turned it down
cold. The Maryland Legislature, whose sympathy was
all for the railroad (naturally, since the canal company was Virginian) pleaded for a reasonable atti-
tude on both sides, and the C. & O. handsomely agreed
to let the B. & O. turn over its unexpended capital for
completion of the ditch to Cumberland, with an
agreement "to abandon for the present, at least, all
idea of a railroad beyond Point of Rocks."

This and other stubbornnesses so irritated the legislature that a move was started to void the canal charter in Maryland, on the ground that its time limit had
run out; the canal company fought this one to a standstill, too. Finally, after nearly two years of bickering,
the compromise was reached: the B. & O. would share
the right-of-way, and in return would subscribe to

2,500 shares of canal stock when it had reached the
Ferry. Even then it is likely that the canal promoters
saw the handwriting on the wall, which was to be
translated by a speaker at the grand opening in Cumberland in 1850 thus: "Thousands have been ruined by
their connection with this work and few for this
reason have cause to bless it." For the stock deal
forced the Baltimore & Ohio to become the practical
owner of an enterprise that had failed, and whose
possession could do it or its stockholders no good.

On December 1, 1834, the first passenger train
pulled into a temporary depot across the Potomac
from the Ferry—just about at the spot where Robert
Harper and Peter Hoffman had waited for Peter in
The Hole to come for them. It had made the run from
Baltimore in six hours, behind the pride of the three-
engine "locomotive fleet," the *Arabian*. Two years
later the river was bridged and the Baltimore & Ohio
stood upon the threshold of its dream: a clear opening
to the Ohio, with a choice of several practicable
routes.

The Ferry's first bridge, more or less duplicated by
others later, was unique. It was covered, nine hundred feet long and with six spans. What made it
unique were the curves in it (in this day of the Golden
Gate and the George Washington, it is hard to imagine a bridge with curves) and the fact that it held
the world's only railroad junction placed in the middle of a river. The Winchester & Potomac, up from the
South, ran along the Shenandoah shore and connected
with the B. & O. in mid-span, at the crotch of a Y. The
Y's left branch went to Winchester, the right along

the Virginia bank of the Potomac to Martinsburg and then to Cumberland.

Now the Ferry had everything a rising young city needed—stable industry, workmen who were faithful even though most of them did drink too much, and a railroad.

It also had the makings of its greatest griefs.

12

And, of course, the village began to act like a city. The everything it had included labor troubles.

The Works had grown and sometimes had a peak employment of three hundred men. This meant much to the Ferry, in the way of business, and of course it meant the usual struggle in a far-off place, namely Washington, for control. Politics never change, nor do the suspicions and envies with which the military and the civilian regard each other. The Works, for which read Harpers Ferry, was no exception.

It was quite a plant when they finished it. Including the timberlands on Loudoun Heights, the government had 1,800 acres. There were 113 buildings, eighty-nine of them dwellings, a superintendent's office, twenty-one shops, two schools, the engine house, and three arsenal-magazine buildings. By 1821 this plant had produced 119,911 muskets, 19,718 rifles, 4,088 pistols, four harpoon guns and (a government

inventory never misses!) 37,750 screw drivers. All of
this had a value of $2,600,000.

Production went well enough under the civilian
superintendents, of whom the first was Perkins, he
of Jefferson's eaglets. A man named Stubblefield was
unjustly court-martialed twice and after his second
acquittal resigned in disgust. A Colonel Dunn, whose
title was nominal, was so hard on the men one Ebenezer
Cox got drunk on equal parts of whiskey and resent-
ment and shot him in the belly; when Dunn died,
Ebenezer, saying to the end he was glad he fired, was
hanged.

Then came the Army, the good old unquenchable
Army. Whatever would we do for production stupidity without an Army!

The government decided efficiency would be best
served by having a little spit-and-polish around the
place. Some was needed, to be sure, what with workmen bringing their lunch in bottles. But an ordnance
officer, Major Craig, who appeared in 1841, was
hardly the one to prove it. Craig made a mistake common to army officers; he decided to effect all reforms
at once. He abolished piecework, forcing carefree
employees to keep regular hours. The magnitude of
this affront was equaled only by wholesale firings for
drinking. At an indignation meeting virtually all the
employees decided something more drastic than a
communication was called for.

So they chartered a canal boat, trundled their kegs
of beer aboard, and set off for Washington. You could
see a President more easily then than now, so it was

no particular trick to get into Tyler's office, where he
was somewhat taken aback when one of the drunker
artisans extended a paw and said, "H'ya, Prez—stick
your corn-stealer thar!" Mr. Tyler listened to the
complaints, said he was unable to do anything, and
suggested the men "go back and hammer out your
difficulties at your own forges."

But Craig was removed and succeeded by Major
John Symington, who was a better diplomatist. His
popularity was great enough, when the Mexican War
came along, for a full company to follow him toward
Chapultepec.

In 1854, after thirteen years of military rule, the
Works went back to civilians. The military, probably,
was as pleased. It had had to deal with much, exempli-
fied well in the case of Superintendent Symington who
was flooded with job applicants of the "Guv'mint-
owes-me-a-livin'" stamp. To one such, a harness-
maker, Symington said tiredly, "Oh, I'll let you know
whenever we start making guns out of leather."

13

And always there were the little people, the ones
who form the red thread, but, where history has been
done, run far too faintly through the tapestry. Here in
the Ferry they had their heroes and their fools, their
moments of high excitement and higher panic.

There was Launcelot, son of General Charles Lee,

who dried up before an audience of five hundred as he arose to make a speech, and was so chagrined he appeared next day wearing an open Bible for a hat. "He lived to be very old and was quite mad," said a tolerant commentator, "but he was ever harmless."

And there was Edgar Fuker who found the cure for cancer: "To hold a frog or toad, alive or dead, against the affected part for an hour, repeating until cured." Edgar said he had disposed of a troublesome nose cancer by this means, albeit in the process he had sent six frogs to their ancestors.

There was the great boxing match between Yankee Sullivan and Bob Caunt, in 1847. No man knows today for sure why Harpers Ferry was selected, except that the fight had to be held in a remoteness due to certain Comstockian sentiments in the cities, and the Ferry had direct rail service to the east. Sullivan was a Cork man, an unmitigated stinker who, in the words of the *Police Gazette*, was "born with a gat in one hip pocket and a pint in the other." Caunt was English, and probably had kinsmen among the armorers at the Works.

Sullivan roared into town, shouting, "I can lick any lime-juicing son-of-a-bitch with one hand behind me," and proved it in the case of Caunt, beating him to an unrecognizable pulp in eight rounds, ten seconds, fighting no rules and bare knuckles.

"They came from the cars like locusts," wrote a contemporary morosely of the New York-Philadelphia-Baltimore sporting axis, an incredible crowd of seven hundred, "the gambling men all dressed in dude clothes and their women got up cheap and fine." Before the fight there were partisan street brawls everywhere, after it a practical riot over payment of wagers. "They filled all the liquor saloons and even picked fights with our people over nothing. We were glad when they got on the cars and went back to the cities."

The trains and the boats arrived and left on schedule, or thereabout. The steamer *Antelope*, refurbished and put on the canal, offered passage to Washington for $1.50, in a twelve-hour trip with meals at a quarter. The Conestogas were still busy, coursing between Alexandria and the West and using Packing Horse Ford; they carried grain and farm produce East and returned with sugar, cotton, rice, English cloth, and French wine. E. H. Carroll opened a hotel to compete with the Wager House, calling it the Opposition, and offered a 25-cent dinner to passengers on the B. & O.: "Roast beef, mutton, veal and fowls; boiled ham, corned beef and chickens; soup and fish in season; with a plentiful supply of vegetables, pastry, fruit &c."

And the famous continued to pass through, some pausing to admire the view, others contributing a moment of high drama, as did Henry Clay when he appeared for a back-platform speech. A man in the station crowd called, "Mr. Clay—I want to tell you something about your boy Henry. He died in my arms at Chapultepec."

Clay cried, "My God!" and went backward into a seat, and then until the train left the crowd stood in full silence watching a father hear of the last moments of his son.

Periodically the cholera raised hell. It was blamed

on a variety of things, including cantaloupe, which were called "cholera bombs," but nobody apparently ever thought of the hogs suffocated in trains and then butchered, or of the unrefrigerated meat which often went through to Cumberland by mistake and returned on a later train with half its weight in germs.

The evildoers continued to go up against the supernatural . . . and lost. A drunken Scot named McFillan decided that the author of an anonymous note to his boss was one Chamberlain. They fought and McFillan died. One Jenkins moved into the McFillan house and invited Chamberlain to a game of loo. As they played a stranger to Jenkins, who saw him clearly, entered and watched a moment. Chamberlain, corpse-gray, croaked, "It's McFillan, back to haunt me," and he could have been right, for a little later he, too, died when a shotgun in a wagon bed went off unaccountably, blowing a hat-sized hole in his back.

And throughout there is the even redder thread, slavery. The country held nearly one-fifth of the slave population of the Western Reserve, just before Brown turned up, some 3,960 as against 10,064 whites. They were well treated, considering, but they were still sold.

In Charlestown an auction saw these prices: one man, $1,200; woman and four children, $1,950; woman and two children, $1,126; boy, 14, $613; boy, 16, $790; two girls, 10 and 13, $795.

Now and hereafter there is little that can be said of the Ferry which will be gay.

It is 1859. A man curiously named John Lynch goes

through the streets on October 8, talking abolition, and is barely saved from living up to his name by the steadier segments of the population.

He is a seven-day caution to the town, which worries so hard about its slaves that it pays no heed to Johnny Cook or the old prospector named Smith.

THREE

the plot

1

The raid on Harpers Ferry was the highest possible point that could be reached by a man and by a village.

We are concerned here with little things. Not with Brown, the Homeric figure of misguided zeal, but a little with Brown the man—and, more, with the men who followed him. For they might have come from the Ferry; they were small-town boys in the main (the average age of his twenty-one raiders was twenty-five years and except for the ex-slave Newby, who was forty-four, all were in their twenties). Some began with a dream and others with a hunger for adven-

ture; all fell under the magnetism of old Brown himself, whose Messianic drive was such that he is a standard case history in the books on abnormal psychology.

So we will place Brown in what a reporter calls a
thumbnail, and then get on with our business of
watching his effect on boys and men and our village.

He was born in Connecticut, in 1800, son of a hard-
scrabble farmer. He was a man as indomitable as the
granite of his own New England. He farmed a little
and was a tanner; he preached a great deal and did not
care particularly what denomination the church was.
He is said to have sworn as a boy to destroy slavery,
even if it meant "carrying the war into Africa." He
went to Kansas and fought the Border Ruffians; he
murdered, or personally directed the murders, of five
pro-slaveryites at Osawatomie in 1856. As "Shubel
Morgan" he went deep into Missouri in 1858, stealing
eleven slaves and successfully escaping with them, by
wagon, over 1,600 miles of frigid terrain to Canada.
There were twelve when he arrived; the baby born
en route was named for him. He had the backing of
many Brahmins in New England, most of whom
piously disowned him for the Harpers Ferry raid.
("Abolition—yes, we demand it! But not—heavens
no!—not by violence!")

The details of all that, and more, you will find in
the history books. If you are really interested, a fine
starting point is in Oswald Garrison Villard's encyclo-
pedic *John Brown: A Biography Fifty Years After*,
whose bibliography is a book in itself.

Of course, the Ferry did not know him much. It had
heard a few reports about rampageous doings on the

Kansas frontier—faraway and not too interesting, to
a bustling metropolis like ours. He was just a name in
the news to the townsfolk until he became a man who
walked across their bridge in the night and by morning had upturned hell for them.

2

In the autumn of the sixth decade of the nineteenth
century, the Ferry had a population of four thousand
with most of the wage-earners safe and warm at the
federal teat. Wages ran to a princely $2 a day. Ne-
groes knew none of the horrors Harriet Stowe wrote
about, and sang as they enjoyed such privileges as they
had. The Ferry's welfare was in the able hands of
Mayor Fontaine Beckham (remember? He had
houses to rent, back a few years, on Herr's Island),
whose stature may be measured by a glance at page
142, Will Book 16, in the courthouse at Charlestown, wherein Isaac Gilbert, his wife, and their three
children are given their freedom forever.

But for all the blazing of its forges and the humming of its machines, our village was still a hick town.
Like the people of hick towns everywhere, those who
could went to the combination depot and hotel to
watch a brand new phenomenon a couple of times a
day. This was the arrival of the B. & O.'s trains. The
villagers gaped at the citified people in the cars, commented on the freight being unloaded, and sought an

involvement thereby with the affairs of a rushing, far-off world. When it came about that a stranger de-boarded—not a drummer, mind, for he would just spend his time in the bar when he was not selling, but a man come to stay—they clustered about him, asking and answering questions, being friendly and helpful, and quite often turning into crashing nuisances. Any newcomer who was moderately clean, was not too pushy, and could hold his liquor was accepted; his Yankee accent would be forgiven, even if it could never quite be ignored.

So here, on the fifth of June in 1858, came young Johnny Cook, carpetbag in hand, a good-looking fellow of twenty-nine. The station loungers took to him at once. He was a Connecticut boy come South, he said, to seek his fortune; he had studied some law but would do almost anything to make his way. All of it was in the best Alger tradition, including the romance to come along in a little while.

He was directed to the Widow Kennedy's, where board was to be had for $2 a week. He quickly found a job in that field where even the passing literate can almost always earn a living, teaching country school. He associated easily with all the classes of the town, drinking moderately and catholically. If he took his noontime's dram at the Wager House, indulging in his standing joke with Isaac Fouke, the proprietor, whereby he would pretend to spill ashes on the rug to see Isaac's spinster sister Christine fly into a rage, he would go in the evening to Chambers' or the Galt House, both conceded even by their habitués to be low drinking places. The quality of his humor there would be less subtle, leaning to bawdy stories and rough practical jokes, which he could give or take with equal good humor.

He made it a particular point to be friendly with Mayor Beckham, who was also the stationmaster, and had, perforce, to be friendly with the porter, Hayward Shepherd, freedman. It was not hard to like Shepherd. He was well- and soft-spoken and one of the town's delights was his running feud with Beckham, a trading of jocular insult for mock insolence which for all its travesty on true democracy was fun to hear. Beckham, by the way, was registered at the courthouse as Shepherd's sponsor, which allowed the Negro to remain in Virginia.

Cook remained with his smelly pupils and their dog-eared books only so long as it was necessary to establish him as a young Jack Stalwart. He had work to do; he may have dawdled a little in its beginnings, for the Widow Kennedy had a pretty daughter, Mary Virginia, and it was good to sit with her in the evenings and make her eyes go wide in admiration with tales of derring-do in Bleeding Kansas, under the terrible Osawatomie Brown. The end result of these tales was as it always will be, to the schoolmiss in the little town and Lochinvar; she became his unresisting adulator, he fell in love with her, and they were married. The record is quite cloudy here, for there seems to have been a child between the marriage in April, 1859, and the raid, in October. It doesn't matter. Whatever else he may have been, John Cook was

a good husband, and when the great plot failed Mary
Virginia tried to follow him in flight over the opposition of her mother and the fury of the town.

And what must he have thought, this young Cook,
when he lay in the deep night beside his softly breathing bride? Of Tabor, Iowa, that Grand Central of the
Underground Railroad, where Brown had first un-
folded his mad scheme to seize a government Works,
arm ten thousand slaves and have freedom at once?
Of his tentative opposition, not from fear, for he had
been one of Brown's bravest in Kansas, but because the
plan was far too vaulting? Of what might happen now
if he wrote Brown and withdrew—the respectable life
he might have, the fulfillment to the Ferrians of all
they now believed him to be? No one can know. But
we can conjecture a little, and we can almost be dog-
matic that Cook could no more escape Brown's
magnetism over the many miles than he had when
the old man sat by an open fire at a Kansas bivouac,
stimulating debate among his men about God and the
Bible, slavery and the peril of war, whether it was
right or not to hug a young girl when tomorrow you
might be dead. There could be love in this darkened
room, in the warm bed with the two devoted young
lying close, but there could be nothing to compare
with that electric force in the leader. His followers
did as they were bid, almost in a mesmeric state. Their
minds might tell them of rashness and they might try
to rebel, as, just before the raid, they did, only to re-
tract shamefacedly when the old man said he would
abide by their vote. But always were the flamboyant
promises of freedom for millions of blacks . . . and

they could clearly be heard in this love-scented room, so that when morning came Cook kissed his wife with half his heart and took the other half out to be about his business of spying.

He quit his job as a teacher and took up the trade of book selling. He had Bibles, a life of Washington, and miscellaneous other things to offer. He bought a buggy and a fair horse. He traveled every lane and road in the county, offering his cloth-bound wisdom and accumulating his dark facts. His customers liked him, even after the raid; although there has to be a Monday morning quarterback everywhere and the editor of the Shepherdstown *Register* played the role with the sour comment, "This same Captain Cook passed here as a literary character and contributed several poetic effusions to the *Register*, some of which proved not to be original." (To treason add plagiarism, as though it mattered!)

Cook's big frailty was his love of talk. He was too bold in his questionings about such quasi-secrets as the slave population; he even asked the county clerk how many Negroes there were when he applied for his marriage license, saying he had a wager to settle. He went into the quarters and talked to the slaves. But he had a personality, the boy did, and even when his garrulity aroused suspicion it was centered upon the person with whom he had talked, as in the case of Betsey Peats. Betsey was a freed slave and, like all those who have left the slums and made good, she dearly loved to visit in the quarters and tell how fine it was in the free outside. She called on some cousins at Hillsboro, about eight miles from the Ferry, and when she had gone they rushed to the massa to quote her:

"That Mistuh Cook, who sells them Bibles and things, he tole me how he got a rifle that shoots twenny shots without stoppin' and can he get his wife and chile safe to Noo Yawk he gonna turn Harpers Ferry upside down."

Betsey, when this comment came to official ears, was thrown in jail and scared white. She was permitted to go presently and thereafter tried not to listen to *anything* white folks said. As for Cook, he was not questioned at all. He was still given the big hello when he went into the Wager House, his wife still looked meltingly adoring when he swaggered into their room. When Aaron Dwight Stevens, most swashbuckling of the raiders, came to visit with his black beard and his beautiful, bellowing baritone, no one counted it strange that he spoke only of outlawry on the Plains. Cook's wife thought Stevens was wonderful, in fact, and giggled when he gave her and little Jennie Chambers pickles between meals. Her mother thought pickles too tart for delicate female insides, but Stevens roared that that was nonsense—anything that tasted good ought to be eaten by pretty girls.

Cook's reports went faithfully to Brown, but he was still so indiscreet that the old man knew of it and was much concerned. In a letter to his chief lieutenant, John Henri Kagi, Brown wrote in August:

I do hope all corresponding except *on business of the Co. will be dropped for the present.* If everyone must write some *girl;* or some other *extra* friend telling or showing our location; & telling (*as some have done*) all about our matters; we might as well get the whole published *at once* in the New York *Herald*. Any person is a *stupid Fool* who expects his *friends* to keep for him that which he cannot keep himself. All our friends have each got *their special friends*, and they *again have theirs;* and it would not be right to lay the burden of keeping a secret on any one; at the end of a long string. I could tell you of some reasons I have for feeling rather keenly on this point. I do not say this on account of any tale-bearing I accuse you of.

For all his indiscretion, Cook was angrily earnest about slavery. He stood, tears of helpless fury in his eyes, in the fringes of a crowd at the Charlestown courthouse, watching a hideous miscarriage of justice: the sale at auction of Charles Manuel, who had committed the high crime of remaining in Virginia after being set free. He read a phony letter in the Shepherdstown *Register*, sneering at it because it was so obvious.

"I'm sorry I ran away. I want to see you all so bad that I don't know what to do. I dream about you all every night and sometimes I sit down and cry all day and all night because I want to come back again. There is nothing here but hard, hard times and bad darkies . . . and I so want to come home!"

So he went his way, furnishing Brown with the statistics later to be found on the war maps and otherwise doing what he conceived to be his duty. He took a job as lock-tender on the canal, for that would keep him close for the call to arms, whenever it might come.

3

And now to Brown, again for the moment, again
sketchily.

He and his followers had met, the year before, in
Chatham, Ontario, and had adopted a constitution for
a new government, with Brown as commander-in-
chief. It was a solemn document, ludicrous in the light
of an attempt to enforce it with an army of twenty-one
men, but containing provisions for the humane treatment of prisoners taken while liberating the slaves
which were followed to the letter in the battle after
the raid.

Brown then went frantically about through the
North, among those righteous gentlemen whose convictions on slavery were so open and whose purses
were so closed. He concluded a contract he had made
with a Connecticut smith many months before, for
one thousand pikes, wicked instruments with a six-
inch iron blade affixed to a stout pole; these, he had
decided in some far-gone solitary moment at his
strategy, would be best in the hands of unschooled Negroes who had, perhaps, never even touched a rifle.

His company was recruited, and it is likely he
expected some of them never to answer his call. He
appeared first in the Ferry in July, 1859, ready to begin
his greatest work.

4

Meantime, what of this company? Who were they? What did they think and feel and fear?

To get a lot onto a little footage, Hollywood uses the montage. It is a good device.

First there was Kagi, descendant of the Swiss. He was Brown's most reliable man, self-taught and brilliant; he was a member of the Nebraska bar, a regular correspondent to the New York *Tribune*, an excellent speaker and as quiet as a happy grandfather. He could in no sense fill Artemus Ward's somewhat biased description, "a melancholy brigand."

Of the five Negroes who made up the raiding party, Dangerfield Newby was the most interesting, the most tragic. His father, a Scotsman, freed him, together with the woman who had borne him; somewhere in his line there was said to be the blood of the Roanoke Island "Lost Colonists." He had married a slave woman and gone North, in due course, to buy or otherwise win her freedom and that of their seven children, so it may be said he was a man of love and tortured by it, rather than an idealist embarked upon a crusade. While he waited for the attack to begin he received a letter from his wife which has survived:

"Oh, dear Dangerfield, come this fall without fail, money or no money, as I want to see you so much! That is the one bright hope I have before me. Buy me soon for if you don't someone else will. The baby is just commencing to crawl."

There were the Coppoc brothers, Barclay and Edwin, who were Quakers, whose mother cried in their home at Springdale, Iowa, just before they set out, "I believe you are going with old Brown again. Oh, when they get the halters around your necks will you think of me!"

The party had its mystic, the Canadian Stewart Taylor who predicted his own death; its atheist, Aaron Stevens, who promised the jailer as he waited for hanging that if there were a hereafter he would return for a visit; its weakling, Francis J. Meriam ("The only positive thing about him was his hatred for slavery," commented Brown), who arrived with $600 and a supply of boatswain's whistles he had thoughtfully picked up in Philadelphia; its in-laws, the brothers William and Dauphin Thompson, whose sister Isabella had married Watson Brown . . . and a variety of others, beginning with the three Brown sons, Owen, Watson, and Oliver, and continuing through Charles Tidd, Jerry Anderson, Albert Hazlett, Billy Leeman, all white and all pretty much like the young men in your neighborhood; and the other Negroes, Osborn Anderson, a printer; Lewis Leary, a descendant of an Irishman who had fought under Nathaniel Greene; John Copeland, born free; Shields Green, who called himself "Emperor."

These, with Johnny Cook, made up the twenty-one. They have been no more than introduced, but you will see them fight and die and (too few) escape.

5

Early on the morning of July 4, 1859, John Unseld
rode from the farm he owned but did not work (he
was retired; tenants and slaves did for him) toward the
Ferry for a holiday dram with his friends. He approached four men afoot, one of about sixty with an
inch-long beard, the others younger. He had no way
of knowing this was Brown of Kansas, his sons Owen
and Oliver, and a Jeremiah Anderson; he accepted
without question, when they had said their good-
mornings, Brown's introduction of himself as Isaac
Smith and the others as two sons named Smith and a
man named Anderson.

They chatted of Independence Day for a while.
Brown, who had warned the others, did all the talking.
Then Unseld, the amenities having been observed,
asked, "Aren't you strangers around here?"

"Yes," said Brown, "we arrived last night. We are
boarding at Sandy Hook."

"Visiting—or do you plan to stay?"

"That depends on how dear land is here. We are
from New York State—far up in the Adirondacks—
and the winters are too hard there."

"Farmers?"

"Stock raisers, mostly. We fatten stock for market.
It can't be done well in the North." Brown paused for
one of those meditative eternities which are essential

to all country conversations. "Might prospect a little, too—you know, for gold or silver or iron, whatever there is. These mountains ought to be rich underneath."

Unseld shrugged. "I was a farmer myself; wouldn't know."

"How much does land bring around here, good pasture land?"

"Oh, five to twenty dollars an acre, something like that."

Brown looked startled. "That much! Lord! we thought we could buy for fifty cents or so."

The landowner laughed indulgently. "You're thinking of someplace else. If you want land that cheaply you'll have to go West—Kansas, some place of that kind."

They meditated again.

"I don't want to be stung," said Brown craftily. "You know how it is. Strangers in a country sometimes pay too much for what they get. But I still like the country. Do you know of anything we might rent until the spring?—then we could see how we like it and we'd know more people and maybe strike a good bargain."

Unseld took a fresh chew and got it well softened. "Hmmm. I don't know about anything that'd go large-scale stock raising—"

"Not that big, right now. Just any place so we can get our things here and settle a little."

"Well, there's the Kennedy place. Dr. Booth Kennedy's, you know—he died not long ago and his widow'd like to sell or rent. It's thirty acres or there-

abouts, with one big house and a smaller one across
the road."

"Where is it?"

Unseld pointed north. "Up the road toward Sharpsburg. About three, four miles. Can't miss it. The big
house is on your right, two stories made out of logs,
and the little one—just a cabin, that is—is across the
way. It's in pretty good shape—Doc Kennedy died
only a little bit ago."

"We'll look."

"I'm coming right back from the Ferry. Will you
take dinner with us?"

"No, thank you. My son here"—indicating Oliver—
"has a little stomach trouble and he's going back to
the house. We'll walk up and look at the farm."

They said their thanks and received their you're
welcome and walked on. Unseld, thinking little if
anything of the encounter, went on into the Ferry;
and if he mentioned the matter it was in the ordinary,
desultory way of a countryman making conversation
about strangers with nothing in particular to distin-
guish them.

The place to which the four walked was constructed
in a fashion usual to the country: kitchen in the basement, living and bedrooms on the first floor proper,
and an attic. It was commodious enough for the raiders, and Brown arranged to rent it until the following March for $35. When next he saw Unseld he in-
sisted on showing him the receipt, probably so that
there could be no question of right to occupy in the
vicinity of the Ferry until the time had come to swoop
down on the Works.

6

Then passed a busy and at times discomfiting summer.
The house was too close to the road, really, and the
neighborhood was curious about the man who was said
to be on the trail of a gold mine, or some such. The
visitors were discouraged, politely but firmly, and so
much so that Unseld never set foot inside the house,
because Brown had refused his invitation to dinner.

The secret was a well-kept one, although there were
close calls. First Brown sent to his home at North
Elba, in the Adirondacks, for some of his women. His
daughter Annie, sixteen, and Oliver Brown's wife
Martha, seventeen, came down to keep house. A gentle old mare named Dolly was acquired, with a wagon,
and nightly trips were made to Chambersburg, where
Kagi had been stationed to handle the "prospecting
machinery," the Sharps rifles and Navy revolvers and
pikes. It had first been intended to have Kagi remain
at the farm but he had been run out of Virginia not
too many years before for advocating abolition while
teaching school at Hawkinstown, and since he was recognized on his first visit he had to be kept in a safer
place.

The story of life on the farm, while the waiting had
to be endured, was told by Brown's daughter Annie
many years later, and since she did it so well there is
no point in rewriting it.*

* Quoted, by permission, from *John Brown: A Biography Fifty
Years After*, by Oswald Garrison Villard; Alfred A. Knopf, Inc.

My father encouraged debating and discussions on all subjects among the men, often taking a lively part in the debate himself. Sometimes it would commence between two in the dining room, then others would join, those who were upstairs coming down into the room to listen or take a part, some sitting on the stairs ready to jump and run back out of sight, if the danger signal was given that some-one was approaching. Although he did not always agree with them, he encouraged them to discuss religious questions with him, and to express themselves freely on the subject. It is claimed by many that they were a wild, ignorant, fanatical or adventurous lot of rough men. *This is not so*, they were sons from good families well trained by orthodox religious parents, too young to have settled views on many subjects, impulsive, generous, too good themselves to believe that God could possibly be the harsh, unforgiving being He was at that day usually represented to be. Judging them by the rules laid down by Christ, I think they were uncommonly good and sincere Christians if the term Christian means follower of Christ's example, and too great lovers of freedom to endure to be trammeled by church or creed. Self interest or self aggrandizement was the farthest thing from their thoughts or intentions. It was a clear case of an effort to help those who were oppressed and could not help themselves, a practical application of the Golden Rule. I heard them ask Father one day if the money to pay the expenses was furnished by orthodox church members or liberal Christians. He said he must confess that it came from the liberal ones. Tidd spoke up and said "I thought so, the orthodox ones do not often do such things."

After breakfast Father usually read a chapter in the Bible and made a plain, short, sensible prayer, standing while praying. (I have seen him kneel, but not often.) This was his custom both at home and at Kennedy Farm. Evenings, he usually sat on a stool in the kitchen because it was warm there, and he once told me he did not wish to disturb the "boys," or spoil their enjoyment and fun by his presence in the living room. He thought they did not feel quite so free when he was there.

As the table was not large enough for all to sit down at one time and the supply of dishes quite limited, Martha and I usually ate alone after the rest were done. She "dished up" the victuals and washed dishes while I carried things into the room and waited on the table. There was no door between the kitchen and dining room then, both rooms opened on to the porch, making a great deal of walking back and forth. After the meals I cleared off the table and washed the dishes and swept the floors of the room and porch, constantly on the look out for Mrs. Huffmaster, our nearest neighbor. She was a worse plague than the fleas. Of our supplies of food a few things were occasionally bought at Harper's Ferry when the men went to the post office after the Baltimore *Sun*, which father subscribed for. Most of the mail was sent to Kagi at Chambersburg—merely for appearance sake. The rest of our food supplies was purchased at the towns and all along the road from Chambersburg down, a few things at a time or place so as not to arouse suspicion. Owen brought a barrel of eggs at one time because they were cheaper than meat. We had potatoes, onions and bacon. Then Martha was an extra good "light bread" maker . . . We had a cookstove in the small kitchen off the porch upstairs, where we did our cooking. We used the basement kitchen and other cemented room on the ground floor only for storing purposes.

The middle room in the second story was used for dining and general living room as the stairway from above came down into that room. The men came down and took their meals at the table, except on special occasions when some stranger or neighbor was calling there. If he or she stayed too long something was carried up the ladder at the back end of the house and passed into the window to the men. Sometimes Mrs. Huffmaster with her brood of little ones would be seen coming while the men were at the table eating. They would then gather up all the things, table-cloth and all, and go so quietly upstairs that no one would believe they existed, finish their meal up there and come back down bringing the things, when the visitor was gone. We did not have any stove or way of warming any of the rooms except the kitchen. The white men, most of them, would watch their chance, when no one was in sight and skulk into the kitchen and stay and visit Martha awhile to relieve the monotony. If any one came they would climb the ladder into the loft over the kitchen and stay there until Mrs. Huffmaster (usually) was gone. The colored men were never allowed to be seen by daylight outside of the dining room. After Mrs. Huffmaster saw Shields Green in that room, they stayed upstairs closely.

I was there to keep the outside world from discovering that John Brown and his men were in their neighborhood. I used to help Martha with the cooking all she would let me. Father would often tell me that I *must* not let any work interfere with my *constant watchfulness.* That others could help do the housework, but he *depended* on me to watch. When I sat on the porch or just inside the door, in the day time, I either read or sewed, to appear occupied if any one came near. When I washed the dishes I stood at the end of the table, where I could see out of the window and open door if any one was approaching the house. I was constantly on the look-out while carrying the victuals across the porch, from the kitchen, and while I was sweeping and tidying the rooms, and always at my post on the porch while the men ate their meals, when not passing in and out from the kitchen with food, or waiting on them in other ways at the table. My evenings were spent on the porch or sitting on the stairs, watching, and listening.

The men did nearly all the washing; we spread the clothes on the fence and on the ground to dry. Martha and I would bring them in as fast as they dried, but Mrs.

Huffmaster would have some excuse to come to the garden, which we had rented before we went there, and then she would notice the clothes and tell us, "Your men folks has a right smart lot of shirts." No one can ever imagine the pestering torment that little barefooted woman and her four little children were to us. Martha called them the little hen and chickens. We were in constant fear that people would become suspicious enough to attempt an investigation and try to arrest the men. The rifles were in boxes called "furniture" and were used to sit on and kept standing against the walls in the dining room, one box of pistols being in one bedroom near Martha's bed. She used it for a stand, table or dressing case, whatever name you wish to call it by. I had to tell people who called that: "My mother was coming soon and that she was very particular and had requested us not to unpack the furniture until she arrived," to account for the boxes in the room.

At Kennedy Farm, my father wore a short beard, an inch or an inch and a half long. He had made this change as a disguise, on his return from Kansas, thinking it more likely to disguise him than a clean face or than the long beard.

Hazlett and Leeman were the hardest ones to keep caged of all of "my invisibles," as I called them. They would get out and wander off in the woods and even go down to Harper's Ferry, going to Cook's home and back in daylight. We were so self-conscious that we feared danger when no man pursued or even thought of it. Watson, Oliver, Leeman and Kagi were all a little more than six feet in height, J. G. Anderson and Dauphin Thompson were next them in height but a little less than six feet; William Thompson and Stewart Taylor were above or about medium height but not quite as tall as the two last. Dangerfield Newby was I think above medium size, spare and showed the Scotch blood plainly in his looks and ways. His father was a Scotchman, who took his family of mulatto children into Ohio and gave them their freedom. Newby was quiet, sensible and very unobtrusive. Stevens and Stewart Taylor were the only ones who believed in "spiritualism" and their belief was more theoretical than otherwise. The latter was nearer to a "born crank" than any other man in the company. He believed in dreams and all sorts of "isms," and predicted his own death, which really came true. He talked as coolly about it as if he were going into another room. He considered it his duty to go to Harper's Ferry and go he did, although he knew he was going to his end. He was all the time studying and "improving his mind" as he called it. He had learned to write shorthand. O. P. Anderson was accustomed to being confined in the house, being a printer by trade, so that he was not so restive as some of the others.

William Thompson was an easy-going, good-natured person who enjoyed telling funny stories, mimicking old people for the amusement of any company he was in. But for all his nonsense he possessed an abundance of good common sense. When the occasion seemed to demand it, he knew how to use it to advantage. He was kind hearted and generous to a fault. Dauphin Thompson was the youngest one of a family of eighteen children. He was a quiet person, read a good deal, said little. He was a perfect blond, with yellow, curly hair and blue eyes, innocent as a baby, nearly six feet high, good size, well proportioned—a handsome young man. I heard Hazlett and Leeman, one day, saying that "Barclay Coppoc and Dauphin Thompson were too nearly like good girls to make soldiers," that they ought to have gone to Kansas and "roughed it" awhile to toughen them, before coming down there. To while away the time the men read magazines, sang, told stories, argued questions, played cards and checkers, studied military tactics, and drilled

under Stevens. When there was a thunderstorm they
would jump about and play, making all kinds of noise
to rest themselves, as they thought no one could hear
them then.

7

There were disappointments. The Northern backers
grew cooler and cooler. The Negroes expected to come
down from Canada never arrived. And then came a
day near Chambersburg, in an abandoned stone
quarry, when Brown knew that he had all the help he
could look for, hearing it from the words of a Negro.
   One of his firmest backers had been Frederick
Douglass, the great Negro writer and orator, who said
in his autobiography that Brown had confided a plan
to raid Virginia as early as 1847, but had not named
Harpers Ferry as his objective. While the men chafed
for action Brown made the dangerous trip to Chambersburg (there were still rewards on his head for
the Missouri raid) to meet Douglass and Kagi.
   The old man outlined the plan in detail. They
would hit the arsenal in the night, arouse the Negroes
in the neighborhood, arm them, and back off into
the hills. He said he had studied tactics enough on a
trip to Europe to be sure a handful could hold off an
army in the defiles around the Ferry. Then they would
strike successive blows, down through the Southern
states, until no Negro would hesitate when a pike was

thrust into his hands, but a great avenging Army of
God would go on the march.

Douglass shook his head, sadly. "You're talking attack on the federal government. You'll array the whole
country against us."

"No, Frederick; they'll rise. Thousands of them
will rise."

"You're wrong. This Ferry you describe—it's a perfect steel trap. You'll never get out alive."

"We will." Brown's disappointment was abysmal.
"We will, Frederick. I'll defend you with my own
life. When I strike the bees will begin to swarm and I
shall want you to help me hive them."

But Douglass was adamant. Dark Kagi squatted on
his heels, chewing a blade of grass, saying nothing. His
dark eyes flicked from one to the other. His intelligence told him Douglass was right; his emotions told
him, right or wrong, he'd follow Brown wherever he
led. And then the conference was over. Brown, usually
ramrod-straight, walked from the quarry with his
shoulders bent. Just before parting Douglass, who had
brought him, asked, "Shields, what do you want to
do?"

The "Emperor" did not hesitate. "I think I go wid
de ol' man." (Only a few weeks later, nearly caught
on a trip to Chambersburg, he was to whisper agon-
izingly in a thicket as the pursuit howled about him
and Owen Brown, "Oh, what a poor fool I am! I got
away from slavery and now I'm back in de eagle's claw
again!")

And there were dangers, but because the country
was somnolent they merely brushed with their dark

wings against the enterprise and went on. There
would never have been a raid, for instance, if John B.
Floyd, Secretary of War, had heeded the anonymous
letter which reached him as he rested at Red Sweet
Springs, in Virginia:

Cincinnati, August 20
   Sir: I have lately received information of a movement
of so great importance that I feel it my duty to impart
it to you without delay.
   I have discovered the existence of a secret association,
having for its object the liberation of the slaves in the
South by a general insurrection. The leader of the movement is "old John Brown," late of Kansas. He has been
in Canada during the winter, drilling the negroes there,
and they are only waiting his word to start for the South
to assist the slaves. They have one of their leading men
(a white man) in an armory in Maryland—where it is
situated I have not been able to learn. As soon as everything is ready, those of their number who are in the
Northern States and Canada are to come in small companies to their rendezvous, which is in the mountains in
Virginia. They will pass down through Pennsylvania and
Maryland, and enter Virginia at Harper's Ferry. Brown
left the North about three or four weeks ago, and will arm
the negroes and strike the blow in a few weeks; so that
whatever is done must be done at once. They have a
large quantity of arms at their rendezvous, and are probably distributing them already.
   As I am not fully in their confidence, this is all the
information I can give you. I dare not sign my name
to this, but trust that you will not disregard the warnings
on that account.

But the disappointments, the dangers could not
weigh against John Brown's obsession: that the slaves
must be freed and God had chosen him to free them.

8

On the night of October 16, there was a "protracted" Methodist meeting in Harpers Ferry, which meant that the godly prayed and rolled until all hours. Brown knew this. He suspected the town would be largely fatigued by its spiritual excesses and would be more soundly asleep than usual. When the day came he found he was right; it rained in the afternoon and that is good for raiders—inclement weather.

He preached at the Dunker church. He walked home with Huffmaster, husband of the "hen" and father of her chicks. Huffmaster told a Senate committee later, "He looked to me only like an old man ready for his bed."

Brown marshaled his soldiers. They loaded the wagon with arms and tools for breaking into places and flambeaux of oak with pitch to ignite them. He had a forage cap he had worn all through Kansas. It hung on a nail in the kitchen. His last act—even after praying—was to walk steadily to the wall, put on the hat, and get it properly fixed.

He went out into the chill, half-misty October rain.

"Men," he said simply, "get on your arms; we will proceed to the Ferry."

FOUR

the raid

1

That which we have been told to recognize as the John Brown Raid began, as far as the people of the Ferry knew, as a shot in the night. Its sound was a faint *splat* against the background drumming of a cold October rain. It came not too faintly to awaken one of the Ferry's sleepers on the instant. His name was John Starry. He was thirty-five years old and the town's most promising young physician. His profession had attuned his ear to the least sound of mankind's many distresses, but for all his alertness, he was a deliberate man and now he lay quietly, listening for a further clue. Presently he found it in a steady panting. He pondered this without arising until he had identified it as something which should not be, the noise of a stationary locomotive on the Baltimore & Ohio tracks, across High Street from his lodgings.

He got out of bed. His great lump of a watch, whose ticking could be so portentous in the stillness of a sickroom, lay on the dresser and, by the light of a match, told him the hour was 1:38 A.M. The panting, then, could be from nothing but the Wheeling-Baltimore Night Express, which must be late.

But what of the shot? There were thousands of rifles waiting for shipment in the warerooms of the federal arsenal, but except for a fowling piece here and there, the citizenry had no arms. There was no occasion to own arms, in the Eastern Panhandle. Its current violences curbed themselves with an occasional grogshop brawl, and the comparatively few slaves were contented and at peace. So, the good doctor thought as he stood staring into the darkness at where his watch lay, there should not have been a shot at this hour. Neither should there have been a cry in the night —or had the cry been the imagining of a mind struggling upward from the dark waters of deep sleep?

He padded to the window in his bare feet. The platform lamps had been put out, making the depot opposite too dimly lighted for train time. The train he had heard was not in its accustomed place but westward of the station, its coaches a darkened bulk against the lighter night, its only illumination the flare from the locomotive's firebox vents. He pondered further. Why was the Baltimore Express standing grimly where it shouldn't be, and what of the shot, and had there been a cry?

He saw two men come to the T-intersection where High Street ended at Shenandoah. They made queer figures, shrouded in what appeared to be long shawls. One carried a rifle. He could see them clearly enough to know that they were not of the town. Low fellows they looked to be, from the country, perhaps, here to drink the night away in the lowest of the town's saloons, Galt's. He watched as the pair entered the armory gate, and found this, too, strange, for Danny Whelan was a faithful watchman and his function was to see that no man entered the gate until morning, when the bell would ring to signify the making of a new contract.

The doctor went back to the bed and sat down. He pulled on socks and pants and stout boots. He stuffed his shirt into his trousers and put on a light jacket. As has been said he was a deliberate man, and even had he known what it was he witnessed, he would not have hurried. He put his watch into his pocket and donned a felt hat. Then, with a glance about the room to be sure he had overlooked nothing that might be of help in this unknown emergency he was about to face, he picked up his black bag and went downstairs.

It was fifteen minutes before two o'clock when he emerged into the street. He paused a moment on the doorstep, looking about him. The shawled figures were nowhere to be seen. The station's streetside platform was deserted, but from the waiting room and from the bar of the Wager House, which shared the depot's roof, came a human gabble more confused than that of a thousand outraged geese.

He started across the street. Three men came to the

armory gate, two of them the ones he had seen from his
bedroom window. As the doctor reached the middle
of the roadway someone opened the door of the waiting room and the third of the strangers roared, "Get
back in there! Interfere with us and you'll get a ball in
your head!"

Starry did not slow his walk. Like all medical men
he had infinite faith in the validity of a black bag as a
passport and as evidence of good faith. Too, he had a
high concept of his oath and his duty; he had heard
men roar before and survived. To be a doctor, by his
lights, went beyond bandaging and pill-rolling to en-
compass calm and courageous example. He knew the
value of his quiet presence when there was no actual
call for his professional skill; by being seen he could
often comfort and this he considered an obligation second only to healing itself.

There were two more shots as he neared the depot
door. Neither increased his pace by so much as a heart-
beat. He had been born something of a fatalist and in
the case of bullets this inherent calm was magnified by
what a veteran of Chapultepec had told him as a boy,
"If'n you c'n hear hit, hit ain't yourn."

The gabble hit him with the force of surf when he
opened the waiting room door. The room was packed
with milling men, all apparently talking at once and
none listening. The passengers from the stalled train
formed little groups that endured a moment, broke up
and reformed, contributing nothing to the night but
confusion. A well-dressed traveler was saying, "It's
those damned railroad strikers . . ." and Billy Throckmorton, the Wager House night clerk, was completing

an anecdote with which he would bore people for years to come, ". . . so when I heard the shot I looked out. One of them spied me and he yelled, 'So you want some too, you son-of-a-bitch!' and he fired, but I pulled back before he could get me. And then—"

Starry stood for a minute just within the door. Andy Phelps, conductor of the night train, came in from the trackside platform. He carried a rifle of great antiquity; its barrel was heavy with rust and its stock was scarred and splintered. Conductor and doctor glanced at each other across the bedlam between, taking quick note of credentials, the black bag and the old rifle. Then they walked toward each other.

"A hell of a weapon," Phelps said, hefting the rifle contemptuously, "but would you believe it, the only thing I could lay hands on in the town. There isn't even a pistol on the train. And one of my people— Logan standing over there by the stove—is carrying ten thousand in cash. The damn fool even went up with Jake Cromwell and me when we went to have a look—think of that, Doc!"

"It was you they were firing at?"

Phelps nodded.

"What is it, Andy?"

"God knows. They've got the government Works, the whole shebang. They've got the bridge and wouldn't let us cross. We were on time, too. Some say there's fifteen thousand in the paymaster's safe— maybe that's it."

"Have they tried to rob your passengers?"

"No. That's funny, too, isn't it? If they're here to rob they could have Logan's ten thousand and Lord knows how much more in money and jewelry." He meditated a minute. Then he started, remembering, "Good God, I almost forgot—they shot Shepherd, Doc. He's in the ticket office—will you take a look?"

They went into the little cubbyhole, with its ticket racks and its strangely silent telegraph sounder, which normally chattered like a mechanical idiot throughout the night. On a bed made of two planks suspended between chairs lay Hayward Shepherd, freed slave. He was on his side, his sweat-bright face turned toward the door, his eyes worse agonized than any Starry had ever seen.

The doctor leaned over him. He liked Shepherd; everybody did. Shepherd carried the baggage and swept the station and tended the stove; occasionally, when affairs of the town kept Beckham from his post, he even sold tickets. He was a gentleman, doubly so with the slaves he encountered as he moved about the town, for his own time in bondage had endowed him with the finest of all compassions.

"What happened, Hayward?" Starry asked.

The tortured eyes rolled toward the ceiling and then back to focus on the doctor's face. "I don' know, Doctuh . . . somebody shoot me but I don' know why."

Starry raised him gently. He lifted the shirt with the ragged, red-stained tear under the shoulder blade, and looked at what he saw. The wound was clean, but big; it needed only one glance for Starry's mind to register a message of the inevitable for the Negro. He let Shepherd sink back gently and winced at the questions the other's eyes asked him, *Why do they*

*do this to me? I never hurt anybody . . . why mus' I
die?*

"Can you talk a little, Hayward?"

"Yassuh. Men on the bridge stop Cap'n Phelpse's
train. He go up to see with Mistuh Cromwell the bag-
gageman. They fire at him and he come back. I said I'd
go and I slip off my shoes . . . When they holler at
me I run . . ."

"Why did you run?"

"I don' know, Doctuh. Jus' skeered, I reckon. I just
wanted to come back an' tell Cap'n Phelps what I
seen."

"All right, Hayward, now try to lie quietly. I'll give
you something so it won't hurt so much."

He ministered, closed his bag, gestured with his
head for Andy Phelps to follow him into the waiting
room. They went from there onto the trackside platform.

"Gone?" Phelps asked when they were in the relative quiet of the outdoors.

"Matter of hours. A big slug, through the lung. It's
still in him—he must be torn to hell inside." A slow
fury began to rise in Starry; he felt that he stood remote from it, watching it well inside him. Phelps
handed him a cheroot and he accepted it and a light
absently.

There came a hail from the gloomy mouth of the
covered bridge. "Hallo, there! How about that train?
Is it coming through?"

"Not in the dark," Phelps yelled. "Not until we
know what this is all about. Who are you? What do
you want?"

"Never mind that. You can come through if you like. You'll find out in a day or two who *we* are."

"If you're here in a day or two," the conductor retorted.

"We'll be here. There'll be thousands more of us, too."

Phelps turned to Starry to say apologetically, "If it weren't for the women and children I've got aboard I'd chance it. Or if they'd let my passengers walk across first. But how do I know about the bridge? Where'd I be if I ran into timbers they'd sawed through and put my train and my people into the river?"

"How about the telegraph?"

"Cut. First thing, I expect. Cut both ways. We might as well be in Africa." He sighed. "Well, I'd better get back to the train. There's weeping and wailing in the cars and it's worse because it's dark. But I'm afraid to light up. God knows what those maniacs out there"—he gestured toward where the voice had come—"would do if I lit up the cars." He looked at the bridge again. "A hell of a business." He went off toward his train, his boots loud and harsh against the gravel of the roadbed.

Starry stood where he was for some time. It would take thinking, whatever he was. He stood until he had smoked his cheroot down to its final inch. Then he went into the Wager House bar, crowded with passengers, and had a single, stiff drink.

2

Bill Williams protected the railroad bridge from
noon to midnight. It was a strange bridge, perhaps
unique: it divided midway over the confluence of the
two rivers to form a Y, the southern arm carrying the
rails of the Winchester & Potomac and the northern
those of the Baltimore & Ohio. It was the watchman's
duty to cross the bridge hourly, checking condition of
rails and ties, and to punch a primitive timeclock on
the Maryland shore.

Williams started his eleven o'clock tour, the last of
the night, grateful that another long trick was almost
over and hopeful that Pat Higgins, his relief, would
not be late. He punched the clock and returned, his
lantern's gleam thrown back by the rain-wet tracks.
For a moment he stood in the door of the Virginia-
side shanty, looking at the sleeping Ferry. From where
he stood he could see the dark bulk of the government
Works, the arsenal where they stored the guns, the
armory further to the west, and almost in a line nearest the river the fire engine house, water tank, and
hotel-railroad station. It was still in the night except
for the murmur of the rain.

Williams yawned and went in to the comfort of the
little potbellied stove and the cup of strong coffee
from the blackened pot. He had just seated himself
on the bench against one wall when he heard the rum-

ble of wheels on the half of the bridge used as a highway. What latecoming farmer would *this* be?

They were on him before he could get up from his bench, men who appeared bigger than they were because of the shawl-like garments and fiercer because of their rifles and the big pistols in their belts. There seemed to be a hundred of them. He was dragged to his feet and shoved out of doors, where he stood confusedly looking about him. His fear ebbed a little when he saw the old bearded fellow, Smith he was called, who had been prospecting in the hills, and young Johnny Cook, who'd boarded with the Widow Kennedy and then married her daughter, Mary Virginia.

"What kind of a joke's this, Johnny?" he asked, grinning.

It was the man he knew as Smith who answered, with so little feeling in his tones that the grin vanished. "You will find it is no joke. Go ahead of us to the armory—and don't make any false moves."

He was prodded with rifle barrels. "Why?" he cried out. "Why do you want to take me? What have I done?"

"You've done nothing, to me. But enough to the poor blacks. I've come from Kansas and this is a slave state. I mean to free all the Negroes in Virginia. I have possession now"—he looked about him and his thrownback head had an eagle's arrogance—"and if the citizens interfere I must only burn the town and have blood."

Williams stumbled ahead of them to the gate of

the armory. Behind it he could see Dan Whelan's white
and frightened face, peering. The sinister men called
for a key and Dan said he had none; the old man turned
to one of his raiders and said, "Get a crowbar from the
wagon and snap the chain."

Then they were pouring into the yard, youngsters
with guns and eager to use them. Whelan, a simple fellow who could neither read nor write, stood con-
founded, his lips moving in prayer. He wondered
briefly what had happened to the two other watchmen,
whose only duty was to guard against pilferage and
fire from the armory forges.

"You will be absolutely quiet," the old man said,
"or you will both be put into eternity."

*High-sounding. Brown was like that. A man poorly
schooled and filled with Old Testament wrath. A man
with the gift of eloquence, whether speaking or writing. A man whose most extemporaneous remarks rang
with something (sincerity? high purpose? fanaticism?)
that remained forever with the hearers.*

The two watchmen stood together, huddled for
comfort, watching the bustle. The old man led several of his followers to one side, gave them soft-voiced
instruction, and returned alone. From what was then
said, Williams and Whelan learned they had been told
off to seize Hall's Rifle Works. Presently five others
listened to orders, climbed into the wagon, and toiled
off up the steep High Street hill toward Bolivar
Heights and Charlestown.

It was then midnight. Billy Throckmorton at his
desk in the Wager House heard the wagon and went to
the door to peer out. He turned to say to Charley

Williams, the porter, "Looks like gypsies," and returned to the desk. Charley dozed on.

On the other side of the bridge, from his home at Sandy Hook, Pat Higgins approached the bridge entrance, lunch bucket in one hand and lantern in the other. He paused to put his key in the clock and then walked under the bridge covering, intent on relieving Bill Williams, for Bill was a man who would get angry over a delay of five minutes. He was walking in the middle of the roadway part of the bridge when he was hailed by three men lounging against the rail. He went innocently toward them and then noticed the rifles. As one approached to seize him he "give him a clout and knocked him ag'inst the others. Thin I ran like hell. But they nicked me on the head and knocked me cap off—but they didn't catch up with me."

Higgins went on to the armory. He had no notion of what had happened, except that it had been lawless. He saw more of the raiders, all wearing the shawls, some carrying rifles and some the ugly pikes.

"I thought thin I'd best wait for the train to be comin' in," he told the audience he at last found in the Wager House bar. "I did. I was standin' outside the station whin they kilt poor Hayward Shepherd, or anyways shot him so's he'll die. What in the name of God are they, anyways? Robbers or what?"

A lounger at the bar said, "Not robbers. Something else, something worse."

"Here to run off the slaves, perhaps?" asked Higgins.

"I think so. Here to run off the slaves."

A little later, as the clock edged toward three, Dr.

Starry encountered the watchman, carrying a crockery
pitcher into the station.

"Water for the poor fella they shot," Higgins explained. "Wait up a minute, Doc."

He was back from where Hayward Shepherd lay in
a moment. He bent his head. "Take a look at me head,
Doc. They're divils, they are for sure."

Starry glanced and said, "Just a crease, Pat. I'll snip
away the hair after a bit and put something on to
keep it clean. Tell me what happened."

"They tried to stop me and I ran. They yelled 'halt'
at me—hell, Doc, I didn't know no more what halt
mint than a hog does about a holiday! They shot and
this is all they could hit of me." He grinned. "I just
seen more of them. I was goin' to get the poor fella a
dhrink when they stopped me again. One said, 'You're
the buck who hit me,' and I said, 'That I am—and I'll
do it again.' They seemed to like me spirit. One said,
'You're just lucky, Irish—I aimed high.' Thin they
asked me for a dhrink and I said I was takin' it to the
poor Nigra they shot an' that seemed to make thim
ashamed, a little. They're only boys, Doc—only boys."

Only boys, Starry thought. Boys with the savagery
of men—or of very small children—and the weapons
to give that savagery point and dreadful purpose. "I'll
see you in an hour or so about your head, Pat," he said,
and went out into High Street. He felt somehow disembodied, a man striving toward comprehension as a
desert traveler might travel toward a mirage. If he
thought hard enough, perhaps he could come upon
motive or reason for this sudden outlawry; but as it
was now, it remained mysterious and horrible.

He saw the two he had first noticed, with their third companion, again at the armory gate. They moved toward him and he backed into a dark corner. They came to within twenty feet of him, but what they were saying did not carry to his ears, their voices were pitched so low. He went around to the track platform and back into the waiting room, saying loudly, "There are three of them right outside. We can capture them and go from there into the armory . . ."

He heard his voice die, as though he had no control over it at all. He had been sure some would join him. But they stood in scared solemnity, in apathy almost. Their silence said as loudly as voices might have, "This is your town. Your town in trouble. You live here. We are but travelers who want only to continue our journey in safety. We want to know nothing about shots in the night or Negroes groaning their lives away in ticket offices or any of the other tragedies that have come to you. This is your town. Whatever it is about, you find out. Whatever is to be done, you do."

Starry turned and went outdoors in disgust. His anger was great enough to make him walk alone and boldly to the very armory gate. As he neared it he called loudly for Whelan.

"Halt!" The order came from the darkness where he could not see.

"Why? Who are you that I should halt for you? Where is the watchman?"

"Never mind the watchman. There are enough of us here to take care of him—and of you, too. You don't want to get hurt, do you?"

"I won't be the one," Starry said furiously. "But

you'll need me." He held the black bag aloft. "I'm the only doctor within reach. If one of you gets hurt I'll do what I can for you—just as I did for that harmless Negro you shot in the back."

He was then within twenty-five feet of the gate, a fine black-haired figure, standing erectly in the half light. The voice did not come again. Nor did Starry speak. He stood during what seemed an endless time of tension, again groping for motive or reason; and all he did was to fuel his anger, to chafe at the inactivity, to want desperately to find the town's suddenly diseased part and by action, as he might apply his surgeon's skill to cancer, cut it out.

He paid yet one more visit to the waiting room. The well-dressed traveler, he who had inveighed against the strikers, was saying, ". . . and it's all Old Buck's fault . . . if Washington would take a firm hand . . ." Starry listened in amused contempt, wondering what it was that went on in the minds of the small and the successful that required them to charge every adverse condition, however remote, to the government they themselves had chosen.

He realized his light jacket was wet. He found Higgins and took him across to his lodgings. He cleaned the scalp wound and applied antiseptic. Then he changed into dry breeches and a greatcoat that would turn the drizzle. It was getting on toward four o'clock and he lay down, dressed as he was, to take a ten-minute cat nap.

3

The second party that had departed from the armory after receiving orders from the old man consisted of Cook, Stevens, Leeman, "Emperor" Green, and Osborn Anderson, the last two Negroes. They rode in the wagon which had brought their arms into the Ferry, four of them walking up the High Street hill to spare old Dolly, who had a time of it dragging the wagon with even one man aboard.

They creaked over the pike, past Camp Hill and through Bolivar to Beall Air, some four miles from the Ferry and three-quarters of a mile beyond Halltown. Beall Air was a rambling old house, with twin wings of frame added to the original structure of brick, the seat of Lewis W. Washington, grandnephew of the illustrious George and a colonel on the staff of Governor Henry A. Wise of Virginia. The house faced south, overlooking a meadow in which bubbled several fine springs, the source for Flowing Springs Run.

Cook drove old Dolly partway up the drive under the tremendous old shade trees and left her there. She stood docilely in the traces, her head bowed against the rain, her horse's mind busy with gratitude that the tug up the big hill was over. Leeman remained with the wagon while his four fellows, working quietly in the dark, found and disengaged a fence rail.

The raiders went to the rear door and without preliminary used the fence rail to batter their way in.

They lit the flambeaux with which they were provided, and moved some fifty feet to the front of the
house, where Washington slept. He was awakened by
the glare of the torches, not having heard the battering ram because of distance and the five walls between,
and sat up startled in his bed. Later he said he was not
so startled as he may have looked, as he believed at
first a late-coming neighbor had dropped in to call.

He had dignity, even in a nightshirt. He was forty-
six at the time, handsome, of medium height, slow and
grave in speech and walk. Friends saw a marked re-
semblance to the Trumbull portrait of his distinguished ancestor.

He got out of his bed almost casually. He looked at
the raiders contemptuously. About the first thing he
said was this: "You're a fine bold set of fellows, I must
say." He glanced at the two pistols in every belt and
allowed himself a thin smile. "A fine set of fellows.
But I doubt your courage. You have far too many men
and arms to take a man alone and in his sleep—and if
I had a popgun I could run you off the place, even in
my nightshirt."

"You are our prisoner, sir," said Cook.

Washington considered him soberly. "I remember
you. You're the book agent. You came to see my guns
last summer and I beat you in a shooting match."

"That was at targets, Colonel. This is more serious."

"Perhaps you will repay my hospitality, then, and
tell me what this means. It is all a myth to me."

"We've come to liberate the slaves of Virginia.
We're both able and prepared to do it. John Brown

holds the government Works now and he wants you."

Washington offered neither remonstrance nor resistance. He began dressing. The men shuffled a little, embarrassedly, as they watched. Cook asked, "You have some guns here?"

Washington did not look up. "You ought to know, Mr. Cook. The inventory you took last summer was a painstaking one. They are all unloaded, however."

"We will have them." They waited in another silence until Washington was ready and then followed him into the dining room, where the fire was still alight. He unlocked the arms cabinet. It held, among more utilitarian weapons, such exhibits as the pistol Lafayette had given his granduncle and a sword sent by Frederick the Great at the end of the Revolution with "From the World's Oldest General to its Greatest" inscribed on the blade. Leeman entered to report that the Washington carriage and farm wagon were ready, the latter loaded with the slaves; he interrupted himself to select a fine English fowling piece as his own particular plunder.

Cook extended the Frederick sword to Washington. "You will hand this to Mr. Anderson there." Washington went red at the insult; Cook remained firm, remembering the moment in the farmhouse, when Brown had told him, "Since Negroes are only *things* in the South, it is proper that we teach them a lesson on this point."

But Cook did have the grace to be embarrassed. "I am sorry, sir, but these are my orders."

Washington ironically proffered the sword, hilt first. Anderson took it. The colonel stood in the silence

for a moment, and then asked icily, "Are there any
further indignities? And what manner of man is it who
can give you such orders—and have you carry them
out?"

"Ah," said Leeman, "you don't know Captain
Brown. Whatever he says you just *have* to do."

"I will take the watch you are wearing," said Cook.
"You will not!"

Green growled deep in his throat. Cook warned,
"Take care, Colonel Washington!"

"Young man, I will speak to you very plainly. You
say your object is philanthropic, but you are no sooner
in my house then you reveal it to be robbery and ras-
cality. I prize my watch. I do not choose to surrender
it. There are enough of you here with enough guns to
take it away from me—but I will not give it up!"

They hesitated, in brief shame. Then Cook by-
passed crisis, asking, "Do you know who Osawatomie
Brown is?"

"I have never heard of the gentleman."

"You must not have paid attention, then, to Kansas
matters."

"I do not, sir. I have become so disgusted with Kansas matters that when I see that name in the newspa-
pers I turn the page."

"Well, you will see Osawatomie Brown this morning. He will tell you what he wants of you."

They went out into the rain and the procession
started. The carriage was in front, the farm wagon
behind it, and the rig drawn by Dolly brought up the
rear. Washington's five slaves, sleepy-eyed, cold, and
frightened, stood in the wagon bed, the whites of their

eyes exclamation points in the darkness. When the cavalcade turned into the pike Washington said, "I am cold. I will walk," and was allowed to do so, under guard of Leeman. The latter tried to discuss the slavery issue with the colonel but gave up after a few sentences; Washington declined to break his indignant silence.

They paused once at another house on the road to the Ferry. Cook was on the point of sending the others into the house when Washington looked up at him in the driver's seat. "Go ahead," said the prisoner scornfully. "Wake them up at this shameful hour. They are desperate people—fit adversaries for men so brave it needs only five of them to overwhelm a sleeper in his nightshirt. In that house, sir, are a new widow and her daughters, Richard Henderson's family. Wake them— if you're infamous enough."

They went on, in abashed silence. They might have seized the body of Washington, but they all knew they could do nothing about imprisoning his spirit.

Midway between Beall Air and the Ferry they stopped again, before the homestead of John Allstadt. Their hammerings at the door brought women's heads into the upstairs windows and shrieks of "Murder!"

Green yelled, "Shut up that God damned yellin' or I'll blow your heads off!"

Allstadt was taken in a downstairs bedroom as Washington had been. John Thomas, his eighteen-year-old son (who never explained, incidentally, what he had done with the hours between the protracted Methodist meeting he attended and 1 A.M., when he

reached home to find his body servant waiting up for
him) leaped out of bed and ran for a shotgun in the
corner. His cousin Hannah Hall, always called aunt,
came into the room in a wrapper and grabbed the
gun's barrel.

"Put it down, John. You can do nothing. I heard
them say to your father that they have an army and it
has seized the government Works. There are a thousand of them in the Ferry and more coming."

"Taking the armory is little enough to do," he said
angrily. "There's only the one watchman." But his
aunt's prudence won over his young blood; he re-
placed the shotgun, dressed, and went downstairs to
take his place among the captives.

The six Allstadt slaves joined Washington's five in
the wagon, and the weird caravan moved eastward
again. They stopped once more and Cook withdrew
into a wood to confer with Stevens. When they
emerged the leader warned, "Take care, now. We may
have a fight on our hands."

The vehicles rocked down the steep grade into the
Ferry, brakes keening against the steel tires. They
passed the express from Wheeling, still far from the
depot, still darkened. They pulled up at the armory
gate and Stevens gave the password, "Number one—
all's well."

Brown was waiting at the door of the little building
which housed the fire apparatus and provided a room
for the watchmen. Allstadt recognized him at once as
the man he had known as Smith; and before anything
was said he found himself thinking, "He's calmer now,

much calmer than when he prowled the station platform waiting for his 'mining machinery.' "

The villain of the piece was courtliness personified.
He ushered Allstadt and Washington through the
door, nodded graciously when young Allstadt asked if
it would be all right to stay outdoors.

"You will find a fire in here, sir," Brown said to
Washington. "It is rather cool this morning." There
was a little silence. Then: "It is too dark to see to write
at this time, but when it shall have cleared off and become lighter I will furnish pen and ink and I shall require you to write to some of your friends to send a
stout, able-bodied young Negro. I think after a while
I shall be able to release you, but only on condition
of getting your friends to send in a Negro man for
ransom."

"Why take us at all? Why not just take our Nigras?"

Brown smiled frostily. "I shall be very attentive to
you, sir, for I may get the worst of it in my first encounter and if so, your life is worth as much as mine. I
shall be very particular to pay attention to you. My
reason for taking you first was that, as aide to the governor of Virginia, I knew you would endeavor to perform your duty and perhaps you would have been a
troublesome customer to me.

"And apart from that, I wanted you particularly for
the moral effect it would give our cause, having one of
your name as a prisoner."

There was no ferocity in the slaves Brown's men
herded into the little room used by the watchmen.
Each was handed a pike and given instructions to

guard the white prisoners. The Negroes handled the pikes in a gingerly, a dreadful way. They kept shooting glances at their white masters, saying with their eyes, "We don' mean nothin', massas—we ain't goin' to use these things. But we skeered—we skeered o' dis fierce ol' man wid de whiskuhs."

It was breaking day. After another conference, Cook climbed into the raiders' wagon, taking William Thompson and Tidd, and headed east over the silent bridge.

The raider had taken the Frederick sword from Anderson, and now he began buckling its belt about his waist. Washington glanced at him ironically. "Symbolism, sir," said Brown, looking up with another of his seldom smiles. "You will get back your sword—when it has served its lofty purpose."

Washington went to the door and looked out at the quiet village. "He talks like a tract," he thought wonderingly. "But this is what we expected. This is why we've had the patrols on the road and looked at every stranger—except the strangers we should have suspected."

And it had, truly, come. This the prisoners quickly understood. What Nat Turner* had started was moving another step toward the unknown and fearful future.

* Nat Turner, slave born in the same year as Brown (1800), claimed to see visions and hear voices from an early age. He became a Baptist preacher with great influence over the Negroes. In 1828 he told an intimate the Voice had said, "The last shall be first," meaning that the Negro would prevail; three years later, taking a solar eclipse as a signal, Turner marshaled a band of sixty blacks and raided plantations around Southampton. In all, fifty-five persons were butchered before Turner and nineteen conspirators were captured and hanged.

4

Twice in the night old Brown had sent messengers
from among his captives to tell Phelps he might move
his train. The first such courier was Albert Griest, who
was seized on the Maryland side by the bridge guard
as he and his son returned from having attended the
protracted meeting. At three o'clock Brown summoned the elder Griest.

"You may go and tell the captain of the train to move
it if he likes."

"What is this about, Captain?" Griest asked. "Is the
town under martial law or what?"

"Never mind that. Just do as I tell you and you
won't get hurt."

Griest carried out his mission, taking his message to
Fontaine Beckham, who passed the word to Phelps.
The conductor stood firm on his decision not to move
until daylight, when he would be able personally to
check the condition of the bridge. Griest, who was
quite old, returned to report to Brown and was told
he might go home. His son was nowhere to be seen
and the old gentleman was too frightened to cross the
bridge to the Maryland shore alone. He spent the balance of the night lurking in alleys and other dark
places, where he could find the illusion of safety in
what seemed to him a world gone mad.

Then, at 6 A.M. with the east streaking coldly
against the drizzle, Phelps went forward to the bridge.

He was met this time by Brown himself. They stood a
wary distance apart and parleyed.

"I've got to move my train," Phelps said. "I have
women and children aboard and your men have frightened them out of their wits."

"I sent word three hours ago that you could go."

"I didn't know the condition of the bridge. I still
don't. I have lives dependent on what I decide, remember that."

"Your bridge is safe. I'll walk with you just ahead of
the engine. You can proceed to Baltimore provided
you promise to hold your peace and say nothing along
the route as to what is going on here."

Phelps laughed outright. "My God, man, are you
daft? I'm almost five hours late. The telegraph's been
out since you cut it. Don't you suppose they know
something is wrong here? They've been able to talk
by telegraph all around us—to Frederick, to Cumberland, to Wheeling. They *know* there's trouble in
Harpers Ferry."

Brown nodded resignedly. "I presume you're right.
Very well, then—move your train and do as you see
fit."

Phelps still hesitated. "How do I know it's safe?"

"You have my word."

"Your word!"

The old man seemed to grow in stature. He looked
even more like the old Bible pictures of Jehovah; the
heat of his outraged dignity came from him like the
glow of a Pittsburgh ingot. "My word is good, sir. If
you knew something of my heart and my history—if I

could tell you all that lies behind my actions here—you
might not then judge me too harshly."

"Perhaps," Phelps was a brave man. "Perhaps. All I
can think is that there is a man dying in agony back
there in the ticket office. You say you came to free the
slaves. You shot this one in the back—and he was already freed when you did it. He did nothing to die for.
I wouldn't be much of a man if I didn't judge you on
the basis of murder."

"That was regrettable. But some men must die if
other men are to be free."

They stood in silence and in distance, for the
thoughts of each were far apart and dissimilar. Phelps
went back to the train, glancing up at Bill Woolley in
the engine cab as he passed. Bill shifted his chew to
another cheek, spat, asked, "Well, Andy?"

"Go ahead, Bill. Move it slow. I'll be right ahead of
you with the old man—he says it's safe. If he's lying
he'll go into the river with us."

He went back to the baggage car to tell Jake Cromwell, the baggage man, to close and lock his door but
to be ready to get out if anything happened on the
bridge. Then, not quite knowing whether he was doing right or not, he rejoined Brown and gave Woolley
a go-ahead with his right hand.

They walked slowly to the Maryland side, the train
following at its slowest crawl. Neither man had anything further to say. When the train had reached solid
ground again Phelps nodded, received an acknowledg-
ing nod, and swung aboard the first coach. Woolley
made the whistle wail.

And now, the news of John Brown's raid was ready to be told to a world which would be stirred, exalted, shocked, outraged, and humiliated.

And a few, a very few, of the men who heard of the insurrection would know that the irrepressible conflict had begun.

Kagi, the loyal, the brilliant "Secretary of War," heard the whistle at his post in the Rifle Works. He glanced at Copeland and Leary, who had begun to show fear, and sat on a wooden box to scrawl a message: "Get over the bridge and into hills. Do not delay. Our purpose is accomplished. The countryside is terrified and the blacks will respond. Pray you not remain in this trap."

He gave the message to Leary. "Pass it to the first of ours and have him get it into Captain Brown's hands at once."

He waited. He never learned of the moment in the yard, when Stevens relayed his message to the old man. He may have sensed but could never know the uncertainty among the raiders then, with the old man apparently paralyzed and unable to plan beyond the simple seizure of the Works, with none of the hordes of eager Negro recruits flocking to the banner.

The answer came back. "Tell Kagi to stand firm."

It was a death warrant. All it lacked was the time, and fate was taking care of that. Kagi and Leary had just nine hours to live.

5

Dr. Starry, who had patrolled the streets till daylight, returned to the stable behind his lodgings and saddled his mare. He rode up the hill toward Bolivar. He did not quite know what he was going to do but he had to find other men with whom to share the meager knowledge the night had brought, the burden he felt had been his alone. On the way up he met Colonel Washington's Negro overseer, who lived in a house of his own at Halltown. He stopped the man, who was leading a horse.

"Rebels of some kind have your master," he said. "Get on that horse and tell Charlestown we need militia over here—fast. If you can find him, tell Captain Rowan it's an emergency."

The overseer did not question him, but leaped into the saddle and spurred the horse. Starry sat watching him until he went around the bend in the road.

He found other willing messengers afoot, armory workmen mostly. One he sent to have the bell of the Lutheran Church tolled in warning. Another was dispatched to the home of A. M. Kitzmiller, in charge of the government Works in the absence of Alfred W. Barbour, the superintendent. A third man was sent west to warn the railroad not to attempt to move any trains. Another went to Point of Rocks on the same mission, crossing the Potomac in a skiff.

Starry rode farther up the hill, crying into wakeful-

ness the residents of the houses he passed. Coming toward him, afoot, was Edward Tearney, already campaigning to be the next sheriff of Jefferson County,
and three workmen employed in new construction at
the Works. Starry reined in to pour out a story of what
he had seen. Tearney looked at him wide-eyed and
then walked on, not speaking. Starry stared after him,
shocked at what he assumed to be apathy, comparing
Tearney's phlegmatic reception of the news to the atti-
tude of the train's passengers earlier in the morning.

But Tearney stopped at the brow of the hill, where
he had a clear view into the village. He watched for a
moment and then came back. "I owe you an apology,
Doctor," he said, looking up to where Starry sat in the
saddle. "When you spoke to me I was sure you had
lost your mind. I was trying to figure how we could
put you under restraint and get you to a safe place for
treatment without hurting you."

It was not long afterward that the courier reached
Charlestown and was received with like skepticism.
Leonard Saddler, a very fat man who later demonstrated extraordinary courage at the Ferry, listened
and then shouted to others on the street, "Come and
help me hold this nigger! He's either drunk or crazy
and ought to be in jail!"

Dr. Starry rode back down the hill. He proceeded
along Shenandoah Street to the little bridge leading
to Virginius Island, and saw John Kagi and his two
Negro subordinates, John Copeland and Lewis Leary,
moving about in the yard of Hall's Rifle Works. He
roused the workmen who lived in the neat cottages on
the nearby mainland and told them what had hap-

pened; they pelted him with questions but, as had been the case throughout, there was little enough he could tell them, beyond what was obvious: that the Ferry stood imperiled.

The Lutheran Church's bell began to toll, first a stroke and then a long wait and then another stroke, each knell seeming more portentous than the last.

Now there was life in the town. Now the rumors flew.

Starry never remembered just what it was he yelled to the faces that peered at him from the windows and doors of the houses he passed. He knew it was as alarming as he could make it—too alarming, perhaps, because only a few came to stand at his stirrup, to look up at him like children awaiting instructions from an elder. He hardly knew what instructions to give for he was, after all, no more than a citizen like the rest. He did ask, of every man who approached, about arms; and he felt a sinking when they mentioned their few shotguns, their birdshot, their old squirrel rifles.

He was very tired from the intensities of the night. He needed one of two things to be able to function— rest or a frightful shock. He received the shock as he was still riding along High Street. Someone halted him to gasp that they had killed Tom Boerley, the grocer, who had become too curious and exposed himself. He lay now in the gutter, fat Tom Boerley, who with his fatter wife had no children but loved them, who gave them candy and then made their eyes to bug by holding a full keg of cider head high and drinking from its bunghole. His face had been bright red from the cold water in which he had washed, when he

turned it toward the armory gate; now it was turning
gray as he waited, unknowing, to be carried to a more
dignified place than a gutter.

And in the armory yard, before the fire engine
house, young Leeman looked at the English fowling
piece he had stolen from Colonel Washington, trying
not to be sick with the realization that his loot had just
snuffed out a life.

The news pumped new strength into Starry. His
orders came crisply now. "You," pointing at a man,
"get to Shepherdstown and tell them what has happened." "You," to another, "do the same at Sharpsburg. The rest of you get guns, somewhere."

"Doc," said a voice from the crowd, "I know where
they store the guv'mint rifles to keep 'em away from
high water."

"Good. If you can get to them without getting shot,
do so."

"There ain't no ammunition," said another voice.

"There's powder in the town. Get out your molds
and have your women start making bullets."

As they hesitated he burst out, his voice high with
near-hysteria from the strain, "Well, for Christ's sake
do something! Melt candlesticks, spoons, anything that
will melt. But don't just stand there and let them tear
the town apart!"

"Sure, Doc," they said. "Sure, Doc—right away . . ."

They dissolved into smaller groups and went their
several ways. Starry rode over to the Wager House and
tied his horse to one of the posts before the lobby entrance. The town had become quiet again; apparently
the killing of Boerley, who had surely not deserved to

die, had awed the raiders as much as it had angered the villagers. The doctor went through the lobby and into the dining room. Throckmorton, the clerk, and Christine Fouke were loading trays with mugs of coffee and plates of food.

The physician ordered coffee and rolls for himself. To eat lightly was in the same category as sleeping; another man, thinking of Boerley and food at the same time, might have lost appetite, but Starry knew too well the needs of the body. You slept when you could find time to sleep, if it were only for five minutes; you ate if the food choked you because the body had to be fed to make it ready for working or healing—or even killing.

He gestured toward the work at the trays when the waiter brought his coffee. "What is all that?"

Without a word the waiter produced from the pocket of his white jacket a scrawled note, in the handwriting of an old man. "You will furnish forty-five men with a good breakfast. Captain Smith."

" 'at's de breakfusses what dey makin' now," the Negro said unnecessarily. "Lot of our folks penned up over theah wid de ol' man."

And himself penned with them, Starry thought grimly. He watched as Throckmorton and the porter loaded a basket, standing mugs of coffee upright in it and placing the trays on top. The clerk was back before Starry had finished eating, and stopped by his table.

"The old devil!" he said angrily. "I gave him the damned breakfasts and what do you think he said? 'I'll pay in due course and I'll want a more substantial dinner for two hundred men at noontime.'" He paused, plucking at his nether lip. "And then you know what? That black bastard Charley Williams, who helped me, wouldn't pick up the basket when I told him to bring it back here. He said, 'I'm as much my boss now as you are. I'll go back when I'm damn' good and ready.'"

"And what did you do?"

"What could I do? The old one with the beard stood there laughing fit to kill. I couldn't *make* Charley come back—not with all of them around me with guns. But I did tell the old one something. I told him right. I said, 'This may be funny to you but it ain't to me. I ain't got no nigger blood in me.' Got away with it, too."

The doctor finished his frugal meal and lit a thin cigar. He glanced at his watch; it was after eight. For a moment he reflected on what Throckmorton had told him, realizing that the reaction of one slave could well be the reaction of thousands and not yet, at this point, understanding that therein lay the weird hope of Brown for success in his foray. He then turned his attention to the matter of reinforcements: it was time something was heard from Charlestown. He began to worry. Had the courier dawdled somewhere or, slave-like, forgotten completely the nature and urgency of his mission?

Pat Higgins' wife came into the dining room, sobbing. Her husband followed her, torn between irritation that she had risked herself in getting across the Potomac and pride that he had a woman so fine she would defy the demons out of hell itself to come to him.

"What do you think of her, Doc?" he asked proudly. "Some damn' fool told her I'd been in an accident and it'd cut off me leg and she's after comin' all the way from Maryland, how in God's name without gettin' shot I don't know."

The doctor smiled at the woman, who tried to smile back. He patted her shoulder. "You had best go home, Mrs. Higgins. Pat will be all right. This is no place for a woman—go home where it's safe."

He went out and mounted, walked his horse up the hill, and spurred her into a gallop as soon as he was on the flat. Charlestown was eight miles away, but he could wait no longer for the help the village so sorely needed.

6

Meanwhile, the expedition led into Maryland by John Cook had been busy and significantly successful.

It was only a few minutes after dawn when a horseman, bound for the Ferry, encountered Cook and his two fellows. He was Terence Byrne, farmer and slaveholder. He drew aside to let the wagon pass. He was turning back onto the pike when the driver called, "Byrne. Wait a minute. I want a word with you."

He halted his horse and waited. He recognized Cook

immediately as the young man who had sold books
for a time and then taken a job as lock-tender on the
canal, after his marriage to the Kennedy girl. He
voiced a civil good morning and waited without particular curiosity.

Cook halted beside his horse and pulled back his
coat to show two revolvers in his belt. "I am very sorry,
Mr. Byrne, but you are my prisoner."

"Surely you're joking!"

"I am not, sir. I am in earnest." Tidd came up on
the other side of the horse, his rifle ready.

"No parley here," Tidd said ominously. "If you resist we'll put a ball in you. Come along now to your
place—we want your Negroes."

Byrne shrugged. "I'll go back. I don't want a ball
in me. I'm not armed, but if I were—"

"You're not armed and that's enough," Cook said.
"Dismount."

Byrne did so. They tied his horse to the back of the
wagon and made him walk ahead. At the farmhouse
his brother, Joseph, waited on the porch, curious
about the unexpected return. As he passed him Terence said in an undertone, "This looks like civil war.
For God's sake be careful—I think they're all crazy."

In the parlor, Byrne—as had so many in those few
hours—demanded an explanation of Cook's behavior.
The harangue he touched off startled both brothers
and made so deep an impression that two months
later, before the Senate investigating committee (one
of whose members, incidentally, was Jefferson Davis),
he was able to remember it verbatim.

"We are operating under a higher law than that of

Virginia," Cook declaimed. "We are obeying a power which for centuries has been proclaimed by the philosophers and statesmen and jurists of the United States and Europe. The law of nature. We think that God, in giving man his existence, gave him the right to breathe vital air, to enjoy the light of the sun, to drink the waters of the earth, to unfold his moral nature, to enjoy happiness."

"I presume," said Byrne when there came a pause, "you're talking about the African slaves in the United States."

"I'm talking about all men. Wherever a human soul exists, that law applies. The meanest slave has the same right to live and attain knowledge that you and I possess. I would uniformly arm the slave and tell him to defend his life and his liberty."

It went on, long minutes of it. The Byrnes listened in stark astonishment. Their sister came in, to stand silently as the torrent of Cook's eloquence raged through the room. The only person to be unimpressed, and to retain the lordliness of the Southern lady in emergency, was a cousin, come to spend a quiet week with her kinfolk. She entered the room, listened for only a moment, and turned to Terence, to ask frostily, "Terence, why have you not cowhided these ruffians out of this house? Why do you suffer them to speak to you in this way?"

Cook's oratorical trance was broken. He seemed to shake himself and to return to the present. He repeated what he had said on the road, "We want your slaves."

Terence allowed himself the first smile since he had

encountered the party. "You may have them—but you'll have to do what I do when I want them. You'll have to go hunting for them."

"How is it they're not on the place?"

"They never are, on Sundays. They went off Saturday and I haven't seen them since."

"Then you'll have to come with us, as a hostage. If you will agree to turn over your slaves to John Brown, he will set you free and pledge himself to protect you and your property."

"That I will not do. I will find my protection where I always have—in the law. And if Maryland can't give it to me I'll go to Washington for it."

"It's your choice."

Byrne went to an inner room for an umbrella. Then they went outdoors again and he climbed into the wagon. The raiders rode toward the Kennedy farm, but stopped halfway, at the little one-room schoolhouse where schoolmaster Lind Currie was trying to hammer learning into the reluctant skulls of the country children.

They stamped into the schoolroom's sudden hush, terrible figures in their rain-darkened shawls, with their rifles and their bristling pistols. The children sat wide-eyed, and their teacher was patently terrified.

"Send them home," Cook ordered. "We need this schoolhouse."

Currie nodded to the children. They scurried out the door, two-legged mice in calico and blue jeans. Currie returned to his desk and sat quietly, waiting for whatever might come.

Cook nodded to Thompson, who went outdoors to

fetch Byrne. Tidd went on to the Kennedy farm with the wagon.

Byrne had one moment alone with Currie. "Don't worry, Lind—it's an abolitionist business and all they want are slave-owners."

"But I own a slave!"

"They don't know it yet. Just forget about it."

They waited for what seemed a long time, Currie and Byrne at the teacher's desk and the raiders standing watchful by the door. Then Tidd returned with the wagon, heavily loaded. The three insurrectionists wrested several big boxes through the door, stacking them under the backboard. When they had finished, they rested for a time and in this interval Currie found courage to speak.

"What are you doing?"

"We're liberating Virginia," Cook replied, grinning. "This," pointing at the boxes, "is the stuff we're doing it with. We have possession of the government Works, the railroad, the telegraph, and we'll have the canal by night. You'll see—we're not at play, schoolmaster."

He turned to Tidd. "You'd better get back. Take Byrne with you."

On the road, Tidd and Byrne met Jeremiah Anderson. Byrne remembered him as having been with old "Isaac Smith" back in July, when the Kennedy farm was first occupied. The prisoner inquired, "What's the news at the Ferry?"

Anderson shrugged. "Oh, those people are more frightened than they are hurt."

"We've heard shooting."

"That just means some of them are resisting us and we're shooting them down."

The wagon went on. The rain came heavier; for a time Tidd and Byrne sat in the shelter of a big tree, squatting in the country fashion.

"You know," said Tidd dreamily, "our captain isn't Isaac Smith any more. He's John Brown—Osawatomie Brown, they called him in Kansas."

The shower passed and the rain returned to its October steadiness. They went on across the bridge and to the armory. Byrne saw old Brown, pacing in front of the engine house; they did not speak. Later, when the more select prisoners were being chosen for confinement in the engine house, Brown singled out Byrne with a courteous, "I want you, sir."

Daingerfield, the armory paymaster, was talking with Dan Whelan when Byrne approached. He was asking about the keys to the side gate, and when Whelan said he had them, Daingerfield ordered, "Hand them over and we'll get out of here."

Old Osawatomie's ears were sharp. He walked to the group, in that amazingly youthful, springy step of his, and held out a gnarled palm. He said nothing. Whelan, after a miserable glance at Daingerfield, dropped the keys.

If he thought anything at all in that moment, Byrne decided later, it was that fear is a queer and unpredictable emotion, and that men are only so brave as the impulses of the instant permit them to be.

7

Bill Woolley pulled his whistle cord and let it scream as he applied the brakes for Monocacy Junction. Andy Phelps was off the train before it stopped, running for the telegraph window. Behind him, from the coach windows, the people watched, some of them wondering if the frantic notes they had scribbled and sown from the train, like clues in a paper chase, would be found.

Phelps slid into the station, grabbed a blank, and wrote the first formal message to the outside world about one of history's great upheavals:

Express train bound east, under my charge, was stopped this morning at Harpers Ferry by armed abolitionists. They have possession of the bridge and the arms and armory of the United States. Myself and baggage master have been fired upon and Shepherd, the colored porter, is wounded very severely, the ball entering the body below the left shoulder blade and coming out under the left side. The doctor says he cannot survive. The leader of these men requested me to say to you that this is the last train that shall pass the bridge either east or west. If it is attempted it will be at the peril of those having them in charge. When daylight appeared we were finally permitted to pass, after being detained from half past one o'clock until half past six. The telegraph wires are cut east and west of Harpers Ferry and this is the first station I could send a dispatch from.

He boarded the train and it proceeded. At the next stop, Ellicott's Mills, Phelps found he was a prophet without honor. There was a reply awaiting him, signed by William Prescott Smith, who as master of transportation was second in command to the Baltimore & Ohio's president, John W. Garrett:

> Baltimore, 7:30 a.m.
> Your dispatch is evidently exaggerated and written under excitement. Why should our trains be stopped by abolitionists and how do you know they are such? What is their object? Let me know at once before we proceed to extremities.

Phelps' reply was angry and specific:

> My dispatch was not exaggerated . . . I have not made it half so bad as it is . . . the captain expects a reinforcement of 1,500 men to liberate all the slaves. I will call at your office immediately upon my arrival and tell you all.

President Garrett was not so skeptical as his master of transportation. He had seen Phelps' first dispatch an hour before the second was received and had immediately wired President Buchanan, Secretary of War John Floyd and the governors of Maryland and Virginia. He told Old Buck in his message, "This is a moment of the greatest peril." Buchanan believed him. So did Floyd.

The wires of the Baltimore & Ohio, which after Phelps' first dispatch served as an intelligence arm of the government, began to hum with news of the raid. Frederick was told, Wheeling, Cumberland. Frederick immediately called up its defenders and offered three companies of militia. Winchester offered one, Shepherdstown two, Baltimore five, Richmond five.

In Alexandria, ten miles below Washington, Brevet

Colonel Robert E. Lee was chatting with a friend in Leadbetter's Drugstore when Lieutenant James Elwell Brown Stuart, of the First Cavalry, leaped from his horse and rushed in to report what had happened. Lee was to proceed at once for a conference at the White House; as they rode toward Washington the junior officer (who is to become "Beauty" Stuart, Lee's ablest cavalryman, but who is now so little known his superior will spell his name "Stewart" in dispatches from the Ferry) briefed the colonel on what he knew. He asked to go along as aide and Lee agreed.

The White House conference was a brief one, in which Lee was empowered to take full command of regulars and militia being sent to the scene. An order went to the Marine Barracks, where there were but thirty men ready for action. Lieutenant Israel Green, pausing only long enough to snatch up a light dress sword in his quarters, marched the Marines to the railroad station, where a special train waited to rush the force to Point of Rocks.

The hour was noon. Government was going into action, in an orderly sort of confusion.

8

But at the Ferry, confusion had degenerated into bedlam.

Starry was back from Charlestown, where he had watched two companies, one uniformed and the other "accoutered as they were," mustered at the courthouse. He had waited until the ten o'clock train from Winchester came in, had seen the passengers ordered off and the militiamen go aboard. He then returned to the Ferry at a fast canter.

He now stood in the protection of the depot's walls, talking with young Henry Kyd Douglas, whose father was head of the company operating the toll bridge over the Potomac at Shepherdstown. Within their view and hearing was the entrance to Galt's saloon, on Shenandoah Street. It and the sidewalk before it were roaring, with drunken men reeling into and out of the bar. The drunks screamed senseless threats at the embattled raiders, fired their guns wildly into the air, engaged in brawls among themselves. A gang from Loudoun County was prominent by the manner in which it clung together; later it was to steal the shoes and garments from the dead and desecrate the bodies.

A town which only twelve hours before had been civilized and sane was now mad and gibbering. A town which had known the stillness of death and the awed fear of the living at daybreak was now a cavern of obscene din.

Save for one spot.

For a long time there had been no sound at all from the armory buildings.

In the watch-house side of the engine house an indeterminate number of citizens huddled. The estimate of the number of Ferrians taken captive between Sunday midnight and Monday noon ranged from eighty down to forty-five; the latter is probably accurate. They had no notion as to their probable fate, but the

majority of them were greatly fearful that the bearded
old man and the fierce youths who followed him
would kill them in the end.

Shortly before noon the train from Charlestown
ground to a halt at Halltown. The Jefferson Guards,
under command of Captain J. W. Rowan, drove
through the thick brush to the shore of the Potomac,
commandeered small boats, and ferried to the Maryland side. The rain was a downpour but it did not slow
the forced march to the Maryland side of the bridge.
There Rowan ordered an immediate charge and
Brown's guards—his son Oliver, William Thompson,
and Dangerfield Newby—fell back, returning the
Guards' fire. In a matter of minutes the bridge was
taken, after a fierce exchange with the raiders in the
engine house, and Rowan marched his militiamen
into the Wager House.

At about the same time, George W. Turner, West
Pointer, farmer, slaveholder, rode into town. He had
heard belatedly there was trouble of some sort and
carried his shotgun across the pommel. He rode boldly
down High Street, not so much impervious to danger
as contemptuous of its unlikely presence, being of that
plume-wearing Southern caste. One of the besieged
raiders drew a bead on him and fired. He was hit in
the throat and pitched into the dust of the road, dying
almost instantly.

Now had been done a killing with repercussions rich
in tragedy. A sister of Turner, told he had been slain,
went mad. And the gentle John Avis (to whom John
Brown bequeathed a pistol on the night before his
hanging "because you have been kind") could not

himself be kind in this moment. Avis, almost incoher-
ent in his rage, cried out to Dick Washington, a cousin
of the captive Lewis and a noted hunter, "Kill one of
the bastards! Get upstairs to fire; I'll attract their attention here!"

Washington went to the second floor of a building.
He had a fine rifle but no bullets; in preparation he
had rammed a six-inch spike into the barrel as a mis-
sile. He waited and presently a Negro appeared in the
open street. It was Newby, driven from his post on the
bridge by the arrival of the Charlestown company.
Washington drew a careful bead. He fired and the
spike hit Newby in the throat, slashing it with all of
the finality but none of the neatness of a razor's blade.
Newby went foremost into the gutter and was dead
when his body stopped rolling.

Poor Newby! . . . *"I want to see you so much,
that is the bright hope I have before me . . . if you
don't buy me someone else will . . . the baby is just
beginning to crawl."*

*And they sold her South, sold her and all the chil-
dren, just as soon as word reached them of the heinous
business in which the husband and father had engaged.*

Now the drunks had a body to intimidate, and one
of a nigger at that. They swept about it in an obscene
and impious dance. Jackknives came out to cut off the
ears and the nose as souvenirs; these members were cut
into small pieces so all the brave ones could have a bit.
Sticks were stuck into Newby's wounds and his body
openings. When the sport palled the hogs came to
replace the men. The first hog squealed at the smell of

death, panicked, and ran up the street. Its fellows gathered about it and gave it moral support. The pack returned, to gnaw at the body.

A mountain man, clutching a bottle in one hand, lurched into the midst of the hogs and yelled into Newby's earless and unheeding skull, "I wish you had a thousand lives so you could die a thousand times, you dirty black bastard!"

Meanwhile, the second nondescript company from Charlestown had deboarded west of the railroad station and waited. Both companies were under command of Colonel John T. Gibson, of the Fifty-fifth Virginia Infantry, but for a time no further action was attempted. Lawson Botts of Charlestown was sent with a small force to cross the Shenandoah above Virginius Island, and to take a position on the far Virginia shore, cutting off Kagi and his little garrison, but other than that nothing was done. The militiamen milled about in a disorderly way, inevitably found their way into the saloons, and in a very short time indeed were, almost without exception, drunk.

Brown now began to realize his predicament. The bridges were gone; he could not see the span across the Shenandoah but he had watched Botts' squad move off and knew what it meant. He had lost one man, Newby, and possibly the three at Hall's Rifle Works.

He summoned a youth named Reason Cross, one of the first captives. He ordered him to go with William Thompson, under a flag of truce, and ask an end to the firing until a parley could be arranged. The two went forth, but had gone less than fifty feet when they were surrounded by militiamen and led to Rowan's headquarters in the Wager House, where Cross was freed and Thompson questioned.

Brown, choosing to believe the first flag of truce had been misunderstood, sent forth a second delegation— his son Watson, Aaron Stevens, and, as hostage, Acting Superintendent Kitzmiller. The second mission failed even more dismally than the first. George Chambers, who ran the village liquor store, fired from an upper window in the Galt House, wounding Stevens twice. Someone else fired a bullet, which was to prove mortal, into Watson Brown. Kitzmiller, zigzagging like a deranged bug, raced for and reached the safety of the depot.

Cross and Kitzmiller were the centers of attention. Cross remarked of Brown, "He has very dark eyes and when he fixes them on you they're as fierce as a hyena's." He was present when they brought in Stevens, seriously wounded with slugs in the chest and side, and he stood for a time looking down at the handsome, bearded raider.

At last Cross could not contain himself. He said, "I'd like to fight you."

Stevens, whose bravery was unsurpassed, grinned up at him in spite of his pain. "Why?"

"Because," said Cross sincerely, "you're the finest built and best-looking man I have ever seen."

Watson Brown dragged himself back into the armory grounds. He returned to the engine house and picked up his rifle. Then for a time he staggered about in the open, until he weakened from loss of blood and went indoors to wait in agony for it to be time for him to die.

For every Virginian who showed savagery, as in the case of Newby's desecration, there were a dozen who proved themselves gentlemen. Cross had been freed once in the morning, when he told Brown his aunt would be worried at his absence and was permitted to go and reassure her; he respected his parole and returned. Joseph Brua, one of the unsung heroes of the whole affair, asked permission to help Stevens and Watson Brown; he half carried the former into the Wager House, returned to find Watson had made his own way to safety and went back as a prisoner. To those in the hotel who urged him to remain free he said simply, "I have given my parole of honor," and he held himself to it in spirit as well as in letter, frequently exposing himself to plead with the townsmen not to fire indiscriminately lest they wound their own.

Billy Leeman, who had returned from the expedition into Maryland for the capture of Byrne and the seizure of the schoolhouse, was only twenty, but had lived a full life. He had served under Brown in Kansas for three years and before that had been known as "wild." Annie Brown wrote of him long afterward that he "was only a boy. He smoked a good deal and drank sometimes; but perhaps people would not think that so very wicked now. He was very handsome and very attractive."

Now he was no longer wild. He had found it stimulating to fight from cover, with freedom to move whenever the situation became hot, as in Kansas. But here, bottled up in a little brick building and witness to the long silences into which the leader retreated, he became what he was—a frightened boy. The fear now grown full in his breast had been born in the expressions on the faces of the "big" prisoners—Allstadt, Washington, Byrne. They wore indefinable looks which somehow stood for right and a confidence in ultimate victory.

He resolved to escape. He acted before his resolution was fully formed. Bursting from the upper end of the arsenal yard, he raced to the Potomac's bank and plunged into the water. Pursuit howled behind him. He swam desperately, hampered by his heavy clothing and harassed by the strong currents. Midway across the river his strength gave out and he hauled himself up on one of the jutting shoals to rest. He heard splashing over the sound of his own breathing and turned to find G. A. Schoppert, a villager, within yards of him.

Schoppert held his heavy Navy pistol high. He approached the islet steadily, sometimes swimming, sometimes wading. Witnesses said young Billy cried, "I surrender," as Schoppert approached, but more than forty years later the Ferrian denied this in an affidavit, saying that the boy pulled knife and pistol and tried to use both.

Inexorably, Schoppert approached until he was within four or five feet of the terrified youth. He took careful aim and Leeman sat frozen, as he might have sat under the mesmeric stare of a snake.

Then Schoppert fired, and the huge ball tore away most of the raider's face.

Two others, seizing this diversion, also chose this moment for escape. Hazlett and Anderson, who had been cut off in the upper part of the government grounds, quit their posts and managed to get across the river.

At about noon the western express pulled in at Sandy Hook. Walter Simpson, baggage master, volunteered to go forward. He spoke to someone at the bridge and was told no train could pass.

The Ferry was cut off. And now, in the gray afternoon, it truly roared.

9

Bravery was all over the place except where it belonged—in a frontal assault on the raiders' fortress, the engine house. The courage of the townsmen, some borrowed from the sight of the armed militia but more from the bottle, had little strength and less direction. The amateur soldiers were quite out of hand; moreover, their officers squabbled. Colonel Gibson, whose strategy it had been to divide the force and send one company across the Potomac for the capture of the bridge, was challenged by Colonel Robert W. Baylor, who was later court-martialed for usurping authority.

"I am senior officer and in charge here," said Baylor stuffily.

"That's just fine, Colonel," Gibson replied ironically. "Now you just get up on your horse and ride over there and capture that old devil all by yourself!"

The citizens, since the killing of Turner, had stayed

close to the building fronts. They fired haphazardly at
the engine house, hitting nothing but brick and the
sodden earth. Inside the little fort Brown set Phil
Luckum, a captive slave who stuttered badly, to re-
moving bricks for loopholes; a near miss sent Phil running from his post, yelling:

"Bub-bub-bub-boss, hit's gettin' tut-tut-tut-too hot
yere fuh-fuh-fuh-fo' ol' Phil."

He made a little tragedy too, Phil did. He got pneu-
monia. A magistrate, never identified, ordered him
flung into the Charlestown jail after the capture of
Brown. There, more from fright than exposure, he
died.

In the town, every man waited for some other to do
something. It remained for a hell-for-leather railroader, E. G. Alburtis, to provide the action—a futile
action, as it proved, for the men Alburtis led found no
support from the citizenry.

Alburtis was at work fifteen miles to the west in the
B. & O.'s Martinsburg shops when word of the insurrection, routed through Wheeling, reached there. He
yelled for his men and they dropped their tools to
come a-running—machinists, car checkers, enginemen,
conductors, brakemen. They listened for only a moment and broke for home to snatch up their guns and
rush back to where Alburtis had assembled a locomotive and a coach.

The Alburtis company left its special train in the
Ferry just west of where the Baltimore express had
lain so long, and charged down the railroad tracks,
ignoring the warnings of the townsmen to be careful
and howling an early version of the rebel yell. Cutting

across the armory yard, it forced Brown and his surviving men-at-arms, together with about a dozen of the
most important hostages, into the engine house, already crowded with fire-fighting apparatus. Two of
Alburtis' men were seriously wounded, six more
nicked.

The railroaders broke down the watch-house door
and liberated some thirty prisoners. They paused
then to care for their wounded. Alburtis turned to
seek support from the Charlestown militia. He got no
response. He then brought up a small cannon his war-
riors had hastily loaded aboard the train in Martinsburg and was about to fire it at one of the three sheet-
iron doors in the engine house when someone called
from the Wager House, "Don't do that—you'll hurt
our people inside there."

Now came another lull. From the Shenandoah's far
shore a rifle sounded, and the few men in the vicinity
of the Hall Rifle Works, where Kagi and his two companions were penned, replied to it. This, it later developed, was a futile gesture by John Cook, who had
crept back through the woods and thought by pretend-
ing to be a large force across the Shenandoah he could
effect a rescue of the Brown party.

There entered upon this disordered stage the one
player who had known his lines from the beginning—
the irrepressible Dr. Starry, who had been general and
spy and Paul Revere for all of the long, long day.

From time to time Starry had tried to get someone
to do something about the men at the Rifle Works. He
knew there were only two or three of them; he could
not, however, seem to assure anyone that routing or

capturing them would be a simple matter. But coincidentally with the assault of the Martinsburg company, he was able to recruit perhaps a dozen townsmen. He sent them to the island, under command of a youth named Tyler, planning to follow as soon as he could report his action to one of the military men.

They approached the Rifle Works, firing as they came. Kagi and the two Negroes, Copeland and Leary, retreated, tumbling down the bank to the river. The raiders began to swim for a flat rock in mid-river just as a group of farmers appeared on the opposite shore, pinning them between two fires.

Kagi, who had "stood firm" against his better judgment, was the first to fall, halfway to the rock. Leary managed to drag himself onto the rock to die. Copeland was untouched and he reached a point beside the body of Leary, just as Leeman had reached the false security of the islet in the Potomac. The deadly minuet in which Leeman and Schoppert had engaged so shortly before was repeated; Copeland lay helpless as Jim Holt, a resident of the Ferry, waded out toward him. Holt raised his pistol and tried to fire it but it was wet and clicked harmlessly. He reversed the gun and was about to club his quarry when Copeland whispered, "I surrender, sir—please don't hit me!"

Holt dragged him ashore, without mercy in the dragging. The other townsmen gathered around and from their throats came the terrible unleashed word, "Lynch!" They had no rope. They were knotting their handkerchiefs together when the doctor returned, still mounted, to ride into their midst.

"We'll let the law do that," Starry said harshly.

He grabbed Copeland by the collar, as gently as he could, and half dragged him to the wall near by. There, with the mare as protection, the doctor waited until one of the officials of the town came to take away the prisoner.

10

Grocer Boerley lay dead in a room with his weeping wife. Farmer Turner lay dead. Freedman Shepherd lay dead, really free at last.

But old Fontaine Beckham, probably the town's most respected citizen, was not dead. He was alive and dreadfully upset. He was the stationmaster and these men had stopped his beloved trains. He was also the mayor and he ought to be doing something to cleanse his streets of this shame that had come upon them.

He was warned repeatedly to stop exposing himself, but he could not stand still. He peeped around corners continually, a short fat man with a face that should have been ruddy but was now pasty and drawn.

At about four o'clock, keeping to what cover he could find, he reached the water tower, nearest railroad structure to the engine house. He peered around one of its supports but could see no activity within the engine house. George Chambers, whose bullets had cut down Stevens, came up behind him, noted that he was unarmed, and said, "Fontaine, you'd better get back. You'll get hurt, acting this way."

The mayor did not reply. He continued to peep. In the engine house, where Phil Luckum was busy cutting loopholes in the bricks, Edwin Coppoc, the Quaker boy, sighted along his gun barrel.

"For God's sake, don't shoot!" one of the captives cried. "He's our mayor—they'll riddle this place and kill all of us!"

Coppoc continued to sight. "I'll just take six inches off the wood and give him a good scare."

He fired. He was not the marksman he thought himself. His bullet caught the mayor squarely in the middle of the forehead. Oliver Brown, standing beside him, aimed at another figure, possibly Chambers', but before he could fire, a bullet from outside struck him, inflicting a mortal wound.

The killing of the mayor brought forward a wrath more terrible than any Harpers Ferry had seen that day. Young Harry Hunter, son of the man who would prosecute Brown and a grandnephew of Beckham, went raging after vengeance. He burst into the hotel parlor where Stevens and Thompson, the truce-bearers, were held. He and Chambers dragged the uninjured Thompson into the street, after Christine Fouke had pleaded that he not be shot there. She was said by some to have been concerned about her rugs, already bloodied by Stevens, but this was an unquestionable libel. Not long afterward she went, accompanied only by a Negro with a wheelbarrow, to get the body of Beckham.

"Let the law take its course!" she protested to Hunter.

"Damn the law!"

Dragging the half-resisting Thompson, the two men came upon Pat Higgins in the street. "Get a rope so we can hang this bastard," Hunter ordered.

"I'll get you no rope. I'm killin' nobody."

They went on to the bridge, a little crowd following. Thompson struggled one last time and his words came clearly to the onlookers.

"Kill me if you will! But even though you take my life, eighty thousand will rise up to avenge me! The slaves will be freed!"

"Die, you bastard!" Hunter put his gun to Thompson's head and pulled the trigger. The body fell between the ties and onto the shoals below. A dozen marksmen on the bank fired at it.

Hunter and Chambers returned to the hotel, determined to lynch Stevens, but when they saw the ghastly wounds in his neck and chest they drew back.

"He'll die by himself. It'll be slower. Let him die!" said Hunter.

11

The early dusk of autumn came and with it a respite from slaughtering. The citizen-soldiers went through the motions of picketing the engine house. The drunks continued to reel about, yelling their empty threats and fighting among themselves. Save for Pat Higgins' wife and Christine Fouke, no woman had been seen abroad for hours.

The living and the dying in the engine house then entered upon the longest night they had ever known or were ever likely to know. The hostages remained well to the rear, behind the fire apparatus where there was some protection. Some of them were still uneasy, despite Brown's meticulous observance of the "humanitarian treatment of prisoners" clause in the Chatham constitution; the more timorous thought he might change at any moment and slaughter them where they stood or sat. The Negroes, of course, were terrified. Whatever happened they were bound to lose —immediately if they disobeyed the Jehovian old man, in due course if they obeyed him to the harm of the whites. The only unit of living calm, in fact, was a dog, a big black mongrel with white feet and a stripe down his back; he had joined the raiders somewhere and remained unconcerned in the midst of uproar and carnage.

From his post at the door Brown watched Colonel Baylor conferring with a citizen. Presently the citizen came forward, carrying a handkerchief tied to an umbrella as a flag of truce. He parleyed briefly with Brown, identifying himself as Samuel Strider (a little later his wagon is to carry Brown's corpse from the gallows), and delivered an offer.

"Colonel Baylor instructs me to say if you will set our people at liberty we will leave the federal government to deal with you concerning its property as it may find most advisable."

The old man listened without expression, said, "Wait," and disappeared. He returned in a moment with a scrap of paper bearing this remarkable message:

Captain John Brown answers

In consideration of all my men, whether living or dead, or wounded, being soon safely in and delivered up to me at this point, with all their arms and ammunition, we will then take our prisoners and cross the Potomac bridge, a little beyond which we will set them at liberty; after which we can negotiate about the government property as may be best. Also we will require the delivery of our horse and harness at the hotel.

Strider shook his head. "They'll never accept this, Captain Brown."

"Then we will have more fighting. I have fought Uncle Sam before and won."

"But now—" Strider gestured helplessly. "You're hemmed in. You've a handful of men and the federal troops are on the way."

The door closed and Strider, his shoulders bent with the weight of a pity he could not suppress, returned to report. The next emissary was Thomas Sinn, captain of one of the Frederick companies which had just arrived. He, too, was a personality. At Brown's trial he testified both for prosecution and defense, returning to make his latter appearance "so that Northern men may know that we of the South are willing to appear as witnesses on behalf of one whose principles we abhor."

He was quite a man. He carried no flag but walked boldly to the engine house door, his arms swinging freely at his sides, to show he was unarmed. He entered the house, standing just within the door and looking curiously about him. The two dying Brown sons lay groaning on the floor and the hostages formed a huddle against the back wall. The slaves, miserable and confused, held their pikes as though they were trying to wish them into invisibility.

They talked, Brown and Sinn, to no more purpose than had the previous ambassador. At one point Brown complained, "You shot my men down like dogs, when they were under a truce flag."

"If you take up arms as you have, sir," said Sinn bravely, "you may expect people to shoot you down like a dog."

"I am entitled to terms," Brown insisted. "I had the town at my mercy. I could have burned it and massacred the inhabitants."

"There are no terms, Captain Brown—none but surrender and military protection until you and your men are properly tried."

"Very well, sir." Brown looked at his sons, at his grim followers, the boys and young men with the high look of death bright upon their faces. "We will die just here, then."

"You assume a great responsibility."

"I have weighed it. I shall not shrink from it."

Sinn turned to leave and paused again at the door. He glanced at Watson Brown. "I'll try and send a doctor."

"You are very kind, Captain. Thank you."

Sinn walked to the Wager House in search of a doctor.

Two or three drunken hoodlums were taunting the supposedly dying Stevens, trying to cow him by pointing their pistols at his head. Sinn drove them from the room with angrily blurted curses. As the last of them hesitated sullenly at the door, Sinn shouted, "Get the hell out! If this man were on his feet and had a gun, you'd all have left by the window!"

He had heard of Dr. Starry's work and went looking for him, but for once the ubiquitous doctor was not to be found. Sinn continued his search until he found a Frederick man, Dr. William Tyler, having a quiet drink at one end of the Galt bar. The doctor listened, nodded, and picked up his bag. The two went together to the engine house, where Sinn waited outside for the examination to be made.

Tyler leaned over Watson. Brown's son whispered, "Please, doctor . . . I've asked them to kill me . . . the pain, I can't stand the pain!"

The doctor gave him a sedative, looked at his wounds, glanced upward at the watching father. "Your son?" Brown nodded.

The doctor paused at the door. "I will come back at daylight and do what I can. But—"

"I know," said Brown unemotionally. "Thank you for your kindness."

Sinn and Tyler walked slowly back to the hotel.

They tried to rest in the engine house. There was no light. Outside they could hear the drunken whoopings. Now and then the men spoke together in the dark.

The groans of Watson and Oliver Brown came occasionally. At the door Stewart Taylor lay dead, the Canadian spiritualist who had said he would die. Only five of the raiders were unwounded—Brown, Edwin Coppoc, Dauphin Thompson, Jeremiah Anderson, and "Emperor" Green.

From time to time Brown would ask, "Men, are you awake?"

"Father," from Watson, "please . . . put me out of this misery." (It was Watson who had said bitterly at the Kennedy farm, "The trouble with you, Father, is that you want your boys to be as brave as you are and still afraid of you.")

"No, my son, have patience. I think you will get well. If you die, you will have died in a glorious cause, fighting for liberty."

"Let me die!" This from young Oliver. "Oh, God, let me die now!"

"Be quiet," said his father. "If you must die, die like a man."

In the stillest part of the early morning, Brown called, "Oliver." There was no reply; no breathing could be heard where Oliver lay.

"I guess he is dead," said the old man, and none who heard could detect the slightest note of feeling in his voice.

12

At midnight the train from the east pulled in, carrying the Marines and Colonel Lee, who had caught up from the detachment at Sandy Hook. The colonel leaped from the train, took one look at the unseemly conduct of the citizenry, and said curtly to Jeb Stuart, "Close the saloons—now."

The Marines formed ranks, under the command of Lieutenant Green. His senior, Major Russell, a pay-master, had to serve under the lieutenant because of regulations; he did so cheerfully, participating in the engine house assault armed with nothing more formidable than a rattan cane.

Lee and Stuart made a swift inspection of the Ferry. They satisfied themselves that the bridge was firmly held and that escape over the Charlestown road would be impossible. They were back shortly after 1 A.M. and Lee conferred with Baylor.

"We can attack immediately," said the colonel. "They still have about a dozen of our people in there."

"Well," Lee considered. "I'll wait until dawn. No later."

The time went quickly. The town quieted, with the liquor supply cut off. The regulars, doing a job they knew, conducted themselves as proper professionals: they stacked their arms and sat or lay in sheltered places, well knowing that in a fight whatever rest you could get beforehand might prove to be the difference between living and dying.

When dawn streaked the sky, there were several thousand people gathered at a safe distance to watch.

Colonel Lee communicated to me his determination to demand a surrender of the whole party [Stuart wrote later]. In case of refusal—which he expected—he would have ready a few picked men to take the place at once with the bayonet.

I, too, had a part to perform which prevented me in a measure from participating in the very brief onset made so gallantly by Lieutenant Green and Major Russell, well backed by their men. I was deputed by Colonel Lee to read to their leader a demand to surrender immediately, and I was instructed to leave the door immediately after his refusal and wave my cap. [It was plumed—he was "Beauty" Stuart even then.]

At the signal, the storming party was to advance, batter open the door, and capture the insurgents at the point of the bayonet.

Brown opened the door about four inches and placed his body against the crack, a cocked carbine in his hand; hence his remark after his capture that he could have wiped me out like a mosquito. The parley was a long one. The only condition on which he would surrender was that he and his party be permitted to escape.

So soon as I could tear myself away from the importunities of the hostages, I left the door and waved my cap, and Lee's plan was carried out.

But there had been an incident at the door. Stuart recognized Brown as soon as he saw him. "Aren't you Osawatomie Brown?"

"I am."

"I had you once, in Kansas, in '56."

Brown permitted himself his frosty smile. "You did, sir, but you could not hold me."

Lee, in civilian clothes because he had not spared time to stop for a uniform, watched from an eminence. Edwin Coppoc, he who had slain Beckham, drew a bead on him but one of the hostages threw up the gun barrel, saying, "That's Colonel Lee of the United States Army—shoot him and they'll tear this place down brick by brick and kill the lot of us with their bare hands!"

The colonel was outwardly calm; inwardly he

seethed. He had offered the honor of the attack to the home guard. Both Colonel Shriver, of the Maryland forces, and Colonel Baylor declined.

"These men have wives and families," they said, not realizing the depth of their insult. "They shouldn't be exposed to such risks. You are being paid for this kind of work—let your mercenaries do it."

Lee is not known to have given a direct answer. But his indirect retort was sufficiently cutting. He sent for Lieutenant Green, gave his orders, took and returned a salute, and swept the local men with a glance that said clearly, "You see? A mercenary, perhaps, but a brave one."

Three of the Marines took sledge hammers and began to batter at the center of the engine house's three doors. But it was too well made, of iron, and it was held within by a stout rope, which gave it too much elasticity for the hammers to have effect. Other Marines went off and elsewhere in the arsenal found a heavy ladder; this, as a battering ram, smashed through the door on the second charge.

A voice sounded inside the engine house: "Captain Brown, I wish to surrender."

"Sir," said Brown, "you can do as you please."

"Please"—it was Thompson—"halloo surrender for me."

Byrne and Daingerfield of the arsenal cried at the same time, "One man surrenders," but the noise was now too great for them to be heard. Thompson stood paralyzed with his fear until someone yelled at him, "Get behind the engine, man, or they'll blow your head off!"

Lieutenant Green was the first man through the opening. Colonel Washington, just inside, pointed to a man kneeling and trying to cock a carbine. "That's Osawatomie there."

The Marine lieutenant fell savagely on the old man. He beat upon his head and arms with the sword, which was too light to be lethal; it buckled on the second or third blow.

A Marine died in the doorway. The others rushed in. One bayoneted Jeremiah Anderson as he cried, "I surrender!" striking him with such force that he pinned him against a wooden section of wall, as a butterfly is mounted in a collector's book. Anderson hung for a moment, gurgling in his throat; then his body revolved, slowly and horribly, until it hung head downward. A drunken farmer came in later to stand for a moment looking at the body; then he spat tobacco juice into the upturned face.

Nearby, Dauphin Thompson also died, his cries of surrender unheeded.

The prisoners taken alive—Brown, Coppoc, "Emperor" Green—were hustled out.

Colonel Washington looked about him, drew on a pair of kid gloves, and sauntered outdoors. A friend rushed up to congratulate him. "Will you come to the Wager House and have a little something?"

"I will, thank you. It seems years since I have had anything. It has been a trying night."

In the engine house, there was the whispered requiem of Anderson's blood, dripping to the floor from where he hung . . .

FIVE

the aftermath

1

Lee was everywhere that morning. The big, the sloppy cleaning-up would be left for the Commonwealth of Virginia, when and if the governor got to the Ferry; but right now, in the urgently pressing hours of the aftermath's beginning, there was still work to be done. The saloon-keepers begged and Lee turned upon them eyes which had the double power to silence, that of the contemptuous gentleman and that of the schooled officer doing a military job.

There was a brief, unseemly flurry from the mob when the surviving prisoners were led off: "Lynch!" they yelled, "Lynch! . . . lynch!" But the colonel

smiled thinly at Stuart, constantly by his elbow except
when he was off on a mission. "Lynch," he said with
contempt in which there could still be forgiveness.
"They're so brave, now that it's light and now that a
dozen Marines did what hundreds of them were afraid
to do all night."

Stuart shrugged. "Civilians, sir. They've been
shocked."

"I suppose. You get a different perspective when
you've seen fighting—" He cut himself off at the sound
of shots. They came from across the Shenandoah and
were being answered by militiamen on the bank near
Hall's Rifle Factory. The two officers waited, alert and
yet relaxed, professional. Like, say, the news editor
when he hears the bells from the wire room that mean
"Flash." A courier approached. "Only a few of them,
sir, and they seem to be gone."

The courier went away. Another man came up,
middle-aged, the reliable sort. Lee had heard his
name, Insull or something like that. "Colonel, they're
still a lot of them over in Maryland—at Lind Currie's
school and on the Kennedy farm."

Lee shook his head. "Get some of the Virginia men
and go over. I have too few here myself."

The farmer, Unseld it was, grabbed his arm as he
turned away. "I've told them all, Colonel, right up to
Baylor, who says he's in charge. They say it's not their
job any more and . . . well, Colonel Lee, we're
scared over there. God knows how many are hanging
around."

Stuart suggested, "I could take a squad or so of the
home guard, Colonel . . ."

"All right, Lieutenant. Do that. Bring back anything you find."

Stuart went off, not quite "Beauty" Stuart now, riding a sorry borrowed horse. Lee watched the mop-up at the engine house.

Brown and the dark aide who was so badly wounded had been carried into the paymaster's office, just west of the engine house. Nine bodies lay in a row —the raiders. The civilians had taken their dead somewhere and Luke Quin, the Marine, was in the station, under a blanket. Lee had guards posted at the paymaster's, not that he feared an escape but lest the prisoners be attacked before Governor Wise arrived on the noon train.

He watched it all, outwardly the quiet spectator and actually the administrator of everything that was being done. We can be omniscient with Lee at this moment because he was too much the Virginian, too seasoned the officer, not to have been thinking that it had come at last, that great rent in the curtain of American unity, and while just beginning no man could tell what it would reveal when it was complete.

He went away somewhere and when he came back they were putting three of the raiders' bodies into barrels. The stowers had gotten whiskey somewhere (they always do, he thought, even if you threaten to shoot them), and they were being crude and vicious about their work. Rigor had set in and when he passed Lee could hear the ghastly creakings of dead sinew and resisting bone as the cursing, sweating men forced a body into the barrel. He turned to remonstrate and a resentful voice said, "Better than they deserve—they're not human, killing people in their beds. Carrion, that's what they are."

He realized that it did not matter too much. United States Army or no, he still had a hysterical populace to reckon with . . . and the dead don't mind.

They were quieting down; they stood in smaller knots in the street and there was not so much shouting. He wished Wise had started earlier. He wanted to be rid of this chore and back to the cleanliness of an Army post.

The eleven prisoners still held by the raiders when the door was battered down went about their separate ways and Lee could find much to admire in them. They had been held for sixty hours in a dangerous place, with a man who might turn homicidally mad (for all they knew) at any moment. They had not eaten. When the final assault came the only safe place they could find was among the bodies piled in a corner of the engine house. Yet they remained, of all the people about, the calmest and the sanest; they seemed to have forgiven Brown even before they were liberated.

The colonel walked over to the Wager House where they had taken young Watson Brown, not yet dead but surely dying. He stood just within the door of a little room off the lobby. There was a man holding a cup of water to the dying man's lips; for a moment Lee was angry, when he recognized Tayleure, the Baltimore reporter. He had little use for the press, as a soldier, and yet he knew that the populace must be told somehow.

"Is that better?" Tayleure asked compassionately. Watson nodded feebly. "What brought you here?"

asked the reporter, and Lee's anger left him; the tone was not that of a workman gathering his materials but of a deeply troubled man.

"Duty, sir."

"Is it then your idea of duty to shoot down men on their own hearthstones? Men defending what they think is right?"

Lee stood still, listening. On the other side of the room, under guard of two Marines, Edwin Coppoc and "Emperor" Green sat, their backs against the wall. Coppoc was listening with the Quaker's calm; Green, who for all his bravado had tried to pass himself off as a seized slave when the engine house fell, was quivering in his terror.

"I am dying," Watson was saying, almost inaudibly. "I'm sorry, sir, I can't talk any more. I just did my duty as I saw it."

The colonel went outdoors again. He heard the wail of the west-bound train's whistle. That would be bringing Wise; he could turn the mess over to Virginia now and try, with whatever success might come, to forget some of what he had seen.

2

Stuart and his detachment encountered the Independent Grays on the road to the Kennedy farm. The militiamen reported no one there and shamefacedly tried to hide their poor plunder—flour, country-cured hams

and bacon, sausage, lard, butter and a couple of pistols
to the man.

The lieutenant rode on. He watched as his men
broke open the cases of "mining machinery." He let
each take a rifle and a pistol as spoils of war. He passed
out the pikes to the country people who had gathered,
at first one to a man, then five, then as many as they
could carry. The pikes became the most vivid of the
contemporary souvenirs and sold so well, to travelers,
that counterfeits began to appear, until finally the
Baltimore & Ohio had to bar their hucksters from the
right-of-way.

But at the farm there was one gigantic find. Brown
had never wavered in his conviction of success, except
perhaps at the very end. And his overwhelming confidence had caused him to carry with him—and to
leave at the base of supplies from which he could not
possibly hold a line—the full dossier on the insane adventure. Letters from Northern backers, maps, the
Chatham constitution, the roster of army and government. Whatever a prosecution could require to get a
conviction for treason was contained in one carpetbag,
left in a corner. Stuart no more than glanced at its contents, and then he carried it personally, to be sure of
its safe delivery to Lee.

They rode back. There were scattered alarms during the day of raids on Sandy Hook and other places,
but when the soldiers rushed to their scenes they
proved false. It was somewhat later that Cook, who was
now at large, revealed how he had climbed a tree on
Loudoun Heights and fired into the village, hoping to
create a diversion and give his comrades a chance to

escape. The return fire had cut a limb to which he clung, and he was hurt slightly in his fall.

3

Henry A. Wise could be called a lot of things, but politician seems to contain them all. He was something of a ranter on the platform and, like the Romans, cut loose with a bell-like "Virginians!" when he had a pronunciamento to make. He was stupid, at least in the Ferry, for he countermanded Lee's order about the saloons, whereupon everybody got drunk all over again, and he ordered all horses seized, which sent many a patriotic farmer trudging back to his distant home and wondering why he had rushed to the defense of the Old Dominion.

The descendants of the good governor will indubitably take me to task for all this harshness, but it can't be helped. My interest is not in Wise, the statesman, if indeed he was, but in a chief executive who tries to handle a situation much too big for him. The best thing that can be said for Wise is that he gave Brown his full due. After the first interrogation he said, "There is the coolest and firmest man I ever saw in defying danger and death. With one son dead by his side and another shot through, he felt the pulse of his dying son with one hand and held his rifle with the other."

Officialdom had gathered and was waiting only for

the governor. Senator J. M. Mason, Representative Vallandigham of Ohio, Colonel Washington, and Andrew Hunter, who would prosecute, went into the little paymaster's office, where Brown and Stevens lay side by side on miserable pallets. The old warrior had been washed and Hunter, who had seen "Isaac Smith" often and passed the time of day with him, recognized him for the first time. Lee and Stuart represented the military, and the colonel offered to exclude the curious who had also crowded in if Brown wished it.

The old man smiled frostily. Exclude people from this, which could be his "greatest and principal object"? Let there be the faintest chance that every infinitesimal instant of his martyrdom not go forth to the world? He shook his head in thanks and Lee bowed slightly.

There was a *Herald* reporter there, who took it all down in shorthand. Mason did most of the questioning.

"Can you tell us, at least, who furnished the money for your expedition?"

"I furnished most of it myself. I cannot implicate others. It is by my own folly I have been taken. I could easily have saved myself had I exercised my own better judgment instead of yielding to my feelings."

"You mean if you had escaped immediately?"

"No; I had the means to make myself secure without any escape, but I allowed myself to be surrounded by being too tardy."

Mason was puzzled. "Tardy? How? In getting away?"

"I could have gone away but I had thirty-odd prisoners, whose wives and daughters were in tears for them, and I felt for them. Besides, I wanted to allay the fears of those who believed we came here to kill and burn. For this reason I allowed the train to pass. I did it only to spare the feelings of those passengers and their families, and to allay the apprehensions that you have got here in your vicinity a band of men who had no regard for life or property, or any feeling for humanity."

"Wait a minute," Mason said harshly. "You killed some people walking quietly on the street."

"Well, sir, if there was anything of that kind done it was done without my knowledge. We allowed ourselves to be fired at repeatedly and did not return it."

"That's a damn lie!" one of the bystanders called out. "You killed Mayor Beckham, and he wasn't armed, over by the water tower there, and you killed another besides."

"See here, my friend," said Brown admonishingly, "it is useless to contradict the report of your own neighbors who were my prisoners."

"That'll do for that," Mason cut in.

"Mr. Brown, who sent you here?" asked Vallandigham.

"No man sent me here; it was my own prompting and that of my Maker, or that of the devil, whichever you choose. I acknowledge no man in human form."

They banged at him for a while, but he stead-
fastly refused to give any information that would implicate or even embarrass his Northern friends. When
the expert questioners paused to draw breath, a Virginia volunteer took over:

"How many men had you?"

"I came to Virginia with eighteen. There were
three others in Maryland."

"What in the world do you suppose you could do
here in Virginia with that amount of men?"

"Young man," said Brown indulgently, "I don't
wish to discuss that question here."

"You could do nothing."

"Well, perhaps your ideas and mine on military
matters differ."

Mason had drawn fresh breath and now took a
new tack. "How do you justify your acts?"

"I think, my friend, you are guilty of a great wrong
against God and against humanity. I say it without
wishing to be offensive. It would be perfectly right
for anyone to interfere with you so far as to free those
you wilfully and wickedly hold in bondage. I do not
say this insultingly."

"I understand."

"I think I did right and others will do right who interfere with you at any and all times. 'Do unto others
as you would that others do unto you' applies to all
who would help others to gain their liberty."

"But you can't believe in the Bible!" Stuart ejacu-
lated.

"Certainly I do."

"Then how about 'The wages of sin is death'?"

Brown looked at him, hurt. "I would not have made such a remark to you, Lieutenant, if you had been a prisoner and wounded in my hands."

Stuart bowed. "I'm sorry. You continue to surprise me."

"I have surprised many men . . . Yes, gentlemen?"

"Have you had correspondence with anyone in the North on this?" asked Vallandigham.

"I have."

"Do you consider it a religious movement?"

"In my opinion, it is the greatest service a man can render God."

Another bystander: "Then you're an instrument in the hands of God?"

"I am, sir. On the Golden Rule. I pity the poor in bondage that have none to help them; that is why I am here. Not to gratify any personal animosity, revenge, or vindictive spirit. It is my sympathy with the oppressed and the wronged that are as good as you and as precious in God's sight."

"Certainly. But why take slaves against their will?"

"I never did."

Stevens, he of the booming baritone and the lusty laugh, Stevens who would die like an eagle in chains, had lain quietly, listening and watching. He had smiled now and again at a secret of his own. Now he said very softly, "The man's right, Captain. I know of at least one Negro who wanted to go back. Let's not lie."

Brown glanced at him. He seemed to fight a little war inside his head. Then he said, "Yes, Aaron. I'm answering too quickly—I couldn't know it all."

The hush in the room, which throughout all this had almost a cathedral quality about it, with Brown and his inquisitors playing the parts of priest and deacons at a rite, was broken by a little hum, gone in a moment. But Stevens recognized it as applause and acknowledged it with a quick sweep of his fine brown eyes around the little circle.

They tried to pin Brown down on his Ohio connections, Vallandigham taking the lead, and got nowhere. He declined to name any advisers and insisted he had gone to Kansas under his own auspices and no other. The examination, in all truth, went the way he wanted it to go; whenever Mason or Vallandigham paused Brown seized the silence to speak to posterity.

"We expect no reward," he told an onlooker at one point, "except the satisfaction of endeavoring to do for those in distress and greatly oppressed as we would be done by. The cry of distress is my reason, and my only reason."

"But why did you do this secretly?" asked a citizen.

"Because I thought that the only way we could succeed, of course."

"Did you expect a general rising of the slaves, Mr. Brown?" asked Vallandigham.

"No, sir, nor did I wish it. I expected to gather them up from time to time and set them free."

Even then, the man interested them as much as his movement. A Dr. Briggs cut in, "Were you in the party at Dr. Kennedy's house?"

"Yes."

"Who lanced that woman's neck on the hill?"

"I did, Doctor. I have sometimes practiced in surgery when it was necessary and there was no one else to do it, but I've never studied surgery."

"It was done very scientifically," Dr. Briggs remarked and then, turning to Mason, "They have been very clever with the neighbors, I am told, and we had no reason to suspect them except that we couldn't understand their movements."

A man who had had a drink asked roughly, "Brown, if you had every nigger in the United States—what'd you do?"

"Set them free, sir!"

"Set them free and sacrifice every life in the community!"

"I doubt that, sir."

"Why, you're nothing but a—" He shook off Stuart's arm, "Let me be, Lieutenant. This ain't martial law yet." He turned back to Brown, "Why you're nothing but a damn' fanatic!"

"And I, sir," said Brown with perfect equanimity, "think you are fanatical. 'Whom the gods would destroy they first make mad,' and you, sir, are mad."

It dwindled off. It was a victory for Connecticut. They could not dent his granite hardness, they could not make him lose his temper, they could not make him fear. They backed away from him, probably most of them knowing the first awe of a human being they had ever felt. It remained for Governor Wise to ring down the curtain with a singularly fatuous statement.

"Mr. Brown, the silver of your hair is reddened by the blood of crime, and it is meet you should eschew these hard allusions and think upon eternity."

It is not recorded anywhere that Brown ever laughed outright, but it is six, two, and even he came close in that moment. He cocked an eye at His Excellency and replied, "Governor, I have from all appearances not more than fifteen or twenty years the start of you in the journey to that eternity of which you so kindly warn me. And whether my tenure here be fifteen months or fifteen days or fifteen hours I am equally ready to go. There is an eternity behind and an eternity before and the little speck in the center, however long, is but comparatively a minute. *You* be prepared; I am prepared. All you slaveholders—it behooves you to prepare no more than it does me."

They went out then and left him. Wise said to someone, "Get wagons and take them to jail in Charlestown."

Lee stared at him in astonishment. "Governor! Send them over that road and they'll be torn to pieces—the horses and the wagons, too—before they get halfway. Let them rest here tonight and in the morning I'll send Lieutenant Green and his Marines to guard the train."

"Very well." The governor glanced at Andrew Hunter. "Let's have a look at those documents, counselor."

"All right, governor. But the people expect to hear something from you."

The governor shot his cuffs and went out to meet his constituency.

4

It had become quite an evening. Reaction had set in and the bravery which had died in the darkness was in fullest flower again, stimulated by the free flow of booze. There was an able eyewitness to this, an innocent victim to hysteria named Joseph G. Rosengarten, director of the Pennsylvania Railroad, who through some militiaman's drunken zeal had spent the night in jail as a suspicious person.

Night was made hideous by the drunken noise and turmoil of the crowd in the village; matters were made worse by the governor's order to impress all the horses [he wrote a little afterward]. The pot-valiant militia fought and squabbled with one another, and only ceased that sport to hunt down some poor Negroes and a drunken fellow or two, who in their frenzy said they were Brown's men.

Tired out at last, the governor took refuge in the Wager House—for an hour or two he had stood on the porch haranguing an impatient crowd as 'Sons of Virginia!'

Wise and Hunter went into the ladies' parlor, where much of the floor space was occupied by sleeping Independent Grays and where Coppoc and the "Emperor" still sat in their corner. Watson had died and his body had been removed. The two officials put oil lamps on a table and began to explore the contents of the carpetbag Stuart had brought back from the farm.

They examined the maps, first. They were all of the South—Kentucky, Tennessee, Alabama, Mississippi, Louisiana, the Carolinas, Florida, Georgia—and had been carefully marked in India ink: attack and escape routes, crosses indicating safe places to hide, the white and slave populations in the margins. There were letters, nearly three hundred of them, many signed by such Northern abolitionists as Gerrit Smith, George L. Stearns, Frank B. Sanborn, Samuel G. Howe, Thomas Wentworth Higginson, and Theodore Parker.

There was a "Vindication of the Invasion, &c." in Brown's own scrawl, which shows that sometimes he must have thought of failure:

The Denver* truse was broken &
1st it was in accordance with my settled policy
2nd it was intended as a discriminating blow against Slavery
3rd it was calculated to lessen the value of slaves
4th it was (over & above all other motives) Right
Duty to all persons in regard to this matter
Criminality of neglect in this matter
Suppose a case
Ask further support

And finally, dirty and barely legible, the scrawl a soldier had found beside where Watson, just a few minutes before, had breathed away his life: "Fight on, fight ever, you Hell Hown of the Lower Regions . . . Your day has come . . . Lower your black flag shoot you dogs you devils . . . Hell and furies . . . go in for death."

* Agreement arranged by Governor James Wilson Denver to end the bloody fighting between Kansas' proslavery and abolitionist settlers.

Hunter read the exhibits aloud. The governor stood to one side and gave them a running commentary. It was manifest to Rosengarten that there was no disposition to be fair on Wise's part, for he "meant to prove a knowledge and an instigation of the raid by prominent persons and party leaders in the North. The most innocent notes and letters, commonplace newspaper paragraphs and printed cuttings, were distorted by the reading and by the talking into clear instructions and positive plots."

The crowd quieted a little. The governor went to his bed.

5

In the morning the mob had a hang-over and was ugly instead of noisy. Lee ordered Lieutenant Green to have his full force of Marines ready well before train time. The militia lined the streets, such of it as was fit for duty, but it would have been of no protection whatsoever to the prisoners. What saved them from a quick noose was Green and his Marines. They were as impassive and deadly as a naked blade and the town knew it.

Brown and Stevens had to be carried to a wagon and then aboard the train. Coppoc and Green walked, with a file of Marines on either side. The mob began to howl as they neared the train and to surge forward, with cries of "Lynch them! Lynch them now!" Wise turned on the platform of the car in which the raiders rode and this time he had dignity; his very bearing brought a hush upon the mob.

"Oh, it would be cowardly to lynch them now!" he said, not loudly, but in all sincerity.

The train puffed off toward Charlestown. History had taken another small step.

6

There had been no proper pursuit of those who had escaped. Primarily because no one knew—until Lee was able from Stuart's find at the farmhouse to put together some sort of roster—how many had been engaged in the entire action. But seven were at large: Osborn Anderson, Cook, Meriam, Hazlett, Tidd, Barclay Coppoc, and Owen Brown. Five stayed together for a time, and Cook among them was the only one caught; Hazlett, who had stolen away with Anderson, was picked up within five days of the raid.

The larger party lurked about the Ferry for an indefinite number of hours, inspired by the thought of a rescue attempt; Cook alone did something. The others merely hid high in the hills and later Tidd told one of Brown's supporters, "Twenty-five men in those mountains could paralyze the whole South, by dodging about and striking small unexpected blows."

The destinies of these men, save the two hanged later, Hazlett and Cook, are of little real importance in the story of the Ferry, but for tidiness' sake may be pigeonholed here. Anderson made his way to Canada and wrote a book about the adventure, *A Voice from Harpers Ferry*, filled with inexplicable inaccuracies. Tidd died in another state of frustration, of fever aboard a transport during the shelling of Roanoke Island in February, 1862; he had particularly wanted to take part in the battle because former Governor Wise was in command of the Confederate defenders. Barclay Coppoc was killed when a train he was riding fell forty feet into the Platte River, through a bridge the Confederates had partially burned. Meriam, feeble in body and probably in mind, served as captain of the Third South Carolina Colored Infantry and died suddenly in 1865. And Owen Brown, to whose courage and great strength the others credited their escape, outlived them all, dying in California in 1899.

On the evening of Wednesday, many hours after the departure of the train for Charlestown, word came from Pleasant Valley, Maryland, that the fugitives had attacked a farmhouse, massacring father, mother, and small children. The Ferrians hid in their cellars and in the Lutheran Church, whose bell gave tongue. Lee, with Lieutenants Stuart and Green who had returned from Charlestown, went hell-for-leather across the bridge. They found everyone asleep, including the family of the alleged slaughter, and it was not until Cook was captured that the officials learned his party actually had tried to enter the hamlet in search of food but had been frightened off by, of all people, one of the drunks staggering home from the Ferry.

On October 22, one William Harrison was exposed

as Hazlett, in Carlisle, Pennsylvania, and on the 25th Cook, famished and against the pleas of his companions, went into a village near Chambersburg and was caught.

The cast of martyrs was then complete, even to the widow-to-be, little Mary Virginia Cook, who never knew what struck her.

The other players took up their roles. Lee went back to Washington on the midnight train, telling a planter friend he met en route, "I'm glad we didn't have to kill him. He's an honest old man—mad, but honest and conscientious."

When the planter, one Corbett, reported this to his foreman and asked his opinion, the slave scratched his poll and said, "I know dat po' marse John broke de law killin' all dem folks. But den . . . even did he . . . don't you think, suh, hangin' him'd be a li'l *abrupt?*"

7

Harpers Ferry had been stricken with a sudden and frightful fever. For a day or two the shock was sufficient to sustain it. Then a delirium set in, which was not to abate until Brown had fallen through the trap and Colonel J. T. L. Preston, in charge of Virginia troops at the gallows site, intoned solemnly, "So perish all such enemies of Virginia! all such enemies of the Union! all such foes of the human race!"

It is a delirium we can quite easily understand, for even at this distance what was truth in the alarums, and what hysteria, cannot be determined. It is enough that both the Ferry and its subsidiary stage, Charlestown where the trial would be held, looked over their shoulders while it was daylight and twitched in their sleep when it was dark.

For Charlestown, it was a preview of the very first days of the war to come. The ladies, God bless them, fell to, playing hostess-mother-nurse to the brave soldiery, sewing five hundred bedticks, listening raptly as their men told of their cool intrepidity in the teeth of a plot to murder and rape, only of course they didn't use the word rape.

The weirdies turned up, those characters who are always at the scene of catastrophe and almost always strangely articulate about it, like Peter Crow, for instance, who wrote the New York *Times* a letter:

Like you i have been to the wars or rather the wars came to me, the devoted city was taken by the break of day . . . the balls whistled past me like hail it would astonish you the way it reverberated back from the mountains it was a caution the yankies as they call them here seemed in great tribulation and ran to and fro . . . they baricaded the doors and waited for the day & night drew its vale over this cene of carnage and of glory all night long the random firing the cars bring up the fresh troops ringing their bell as they came to the bridge & the darkness of the night gave it a most funeral aspect . . . i chased a hog off a dead negro in the street . . . the redoubtable cook scared the children out of scool with his dark army, aye said the master they turned the scool into an armaury . . . cook beheld the battle from the pinnacle

tis said tears rooled down his cheeks. [Of the dead] none
to give a cup of water but the showers of heaven, no
priest to hold the cross over the dying penitent, he seemed
to be in a delitious sensation and at times closed his eyes
to console him, he could hear the music . . .

   i have put nothing here but i have recognized myself
or the prissoners, respectable and intelligent men, have
told me as an impartial historian it grieves me to state that
some of the soldiers ran, tell it not in new york, tell it not
in washington.

   i have no time to corect and condence this artickle.

   Virginia law specified that a person accused of treason might be placed on trial within ten days of his
crime. Since court was sitting, it was decided to try
Brown immediately, or one week after the raid. This
aroused a fearful uproar in the North, whose people
screamed of the poor man's wounds and the fact that
he would have to be carried in on a litter. They said
this was lynch law; the temper should be given a chance
to cool before anything was done. To which the answer was simple and obvious: Brown had committed
not one but four murders, as directing genius of the
foray: Boerley, Hunter, Shepherd, Beckham, to say
nothing of the Marine. The first four died without
warning and without knowing why they died. The
Marine was at his work, so Virginia could and did put
him aside in a special class. As for the rest, Virginia
wondered aloud what further consideration might be
expected for old Osawatomie—his trial would be a fair
one and he would be given seven days in which to prepare his defense, seven days longer than any of his
victims had enjoyed.

What the Virginians knew, but only in a dim way, was that this was the "irrepressible conflict" the hotheads of both sides had been talking about so long. The North was blinded by its convictions against slavery, the South was both frightened and courageous. There came a stop in its heart every time it thought of the slave uprising that might have been; but to balance this was the rose-and-plume defense of a principle which was to carry Virginia through four years of bitter defeats, each more bitter than the last.

We must lap-dissolve here again, giving the picture of Charlestown in the period—from the arrests, through the trial, and for the month between sentence and execution. It is strange but true that in those five weeks there was really only one oasis of peace in all the South, and that oasis was one cell in the Jefferson County jail. There Brown sat day after day, writing to his friends, writing to his family—always writing and with no other end (save, true, in the case of his wife and children) than to further the cause for which he was soon to die.

There were other letters written and letters received.

Copeland, having been saved from death by Dr. Starry and now waiting to die at the end of a rope, wrote his parents:

My fate, as far as man can seal it, is sealed, but let this not occasion you any misery, for remember the cause in which I was engaged, remember that it was a Holy Cause, one in which men who in every point of view better than

I am have suffered and died, remember that if I die I die
to liberate a few of my poor and opress people from my
condition of serveatude.

And Brown received one, dated October 20 and
mailed in Chattanooga:

JOHN BROWN:—SIR,—Altho' vengeance is not
mine, I confess that I do feel gratified that you were
stopped in your fiendish career at Harpers Ferry, with
the loss of your two sons, you can now appreciate my
distress in Kansas when you then and there entered my
house at midnight and arrested my Husband and two
boys, and took them out of the yard and in cold blood
shot them dead in my hearing, you cant say you done it
to free slaves, we had no slaves and never expected to own
one, but has only made me a poor disconsolate widow
with helpless children, while I feel for your folly I do
hope and trust that you will meet your just reward. O
how it pained my heart to hear the dying groans of my
Husband & children, if this scrawl gives you any conso-
lation you are welcome to it.
                                              MAHALA DOYLE
    N.B. My son John Doyle, whose life I beged of you, is
now grown up and is very desirous to be at Charlestown
on the day of your execution, would certainly be there
if his means would permit it that he might adjust the rope
around your neck if Governor Wise would permit it.

But peace was confined to this single cell. Elsewhere, starting in the Ferry and seeping on down
south, there was nothing but alarms, coming on the
hour, it seemed; the wires of the B. & O. hummed with
descriptions of sinister strangers, with warnings of
plots in Ohio, and with crisp orders calculated to shut
off the railroad as any possible avenue for a rescuing
(and avenging?) army.

Mayor Thomas C. Green, of Charlestown, issued a proclamation ordering strangers out of town. The mayors of Shepherdstown, Bolivar, and Middleway followed suit; a town council acted for Harpers Ferry, since the foolish bullet of a boy had deprived it of a mayor. The proclamation was enforced to the hilt. Four members of Congress, eastbound on a B. & O. train, spoke too sympathetically of Brown and were hauled off to the Charlestown jail. Three bibulous Cincinnati businessmen were equally indiscreet and suffered the same inconvenience. Proslavery newspapermen were denied tickets to Harpers Ferry by the railroad at Baltimore. The press, in fact, had a tough time of it all around. Most of the reporters had to hire local stool pigeons, but a couple of the more enterprising—Gallagher of the New York *Herald* and a free lance named Orcutt—spent the whole five weeks on the scene. Gallagher had the cards nicely stacked for him: a cousin was on the Charlestown *Times-Democrat*, and got him a job as an extra jail guard. Orcutt managed to slither through the cordon by enlisting in the Virginia volunteers.

The grapevine alarms were almost as loud as that of the courthouse, which rang wildly many times after the first, when the raid was reported as an attack on the Ferry. A huge rescue army of more than five hundred was said to be marshaling at the Ohio, opposite Wheeling, and the railroad spent a lot of telegraph time discussing this. Higginson, in Boston, came up with an idea to charter a tug, faster than anything in Virginia waters, and kidnap Wise, holding him on the high seas as a hostage for Brown. The jailers were or-

dered to shoot Brown and the others in their cells
at the first sign of a rescue attempt. A detective went
to Oberlin, Ohio, to find John Brown, Jr., and did,
actually sharing a bed with him in a country inn; he
returned the report that small groups of men were going to be formed in the neighborhood of Benwood,
Ohio, where at a signal they would seize a train, ride
it to within a few miles of Charlestown and rescue
Brown in the same sort of raid he had conducted.

It went on, until three thousand militiamen were
quartered in the town. They strutted in their dress
uniforms and posed for the daguerreotype men who
turned up from somewhere. They took quick offense
at infringements on their rank. ("They are trying to
form companies for defense," Lee had reported, "but
their material is not very tractable since all hands
want to be captains.") With thousands of them on
hand, it is small wonder that the citizenry panicked
at nothing. A shooting star was called an omen, as were
strange celestial lights, which proved to be the reflec-
tions of a series of barn fires doubtless set by black
and white sympathizers. Pickets fired on a train of the
Winchester & Northern, having heard it was
crowded with bloodthirsty abolitionists. A company
was turned out by marching feet in a field; its gunfire
did nothing but curdle the milk in the udder of Mr.
Ranson's cow, which had wandered into a corn field.
Throughout the nights, whenever a new panic would
arise, the drums would roll and the fifes shrill and
youngsters would come tumbling into the street but-
toning up their pants and buckling on their accouter-
ments. Improperly stacked arms, in a home used as a

billet, collapsed and set a drum rolling down the stairs; this made so much noise other companies were on duty all night, with artillerymen standing by their pieces, lanyards in hand, at the corners of the courthouse.

As the day for the execution neared, President Garrett of the B. & O. and Prosecutor Hunter agreed to limit passengers deboarding at Harpers Ferry to one thousand, half from the East and half from the West. None could get off a train without credentials signed by the railroad and countersigned by the military. All passengers, for the last few days of Brown's life, were warned that cannon and the guns of 1,500 soldiers were trained upon them from the time the trains entered the Harpers Ferry limits until they left.

Wise got hundreds of letters, about equally divided between the denunciatory and the laudatory. In one a Middle Western preacher offered to take Brown's place on the scaffold; he got a witty reply from the governor to the effect that the law made no such provision, but if he just wanted to be hanged and would come to Virginia he could be accommodated.

And when it was all over they counted up, as men must. The estimated loss in forced sales of slaves to more Southerly states was ten millions. The actual cost of handling Brown, much of it for the home guards' transportation, feeding, and wages, came to $287,-459.10.

8

John Brown's trial opened on October 25, 1859. He
was charged with treason, conspiring with slaves, and
murder. The North hollered its head off because he
was tried while lying on a litter, but those who
watched him carried through the streets were sure he
was strong enough to walk. He was no mean public
relations man, that Brown, and in the month left to
him he performed in a way that would make Carl
Byoir himself proud.

I am not going into all the legal mumbo-jumbo of
the trial, since this is not that kind of a book. Instead I
would rather look into the courtroom at a high point
or two, and try to keep the lens trained on those outside, the people who still didn't know what they were
in for as a result of the raid. Such, for instance, as the
town belle, who wrote letters to her friends about the
excitement:

Sunday [preceding the trial's opening] was just like a
weekday; except for morning service you would not have
known it was Sunday at all. At 2 o'clock a dispatch announced that Governor Wise and 500 men would soon
arrive, so that Jefferson Guards and the Alexandria Rifle-
men marched out to meet them. The governor arrived
with 250 men, leaving the same number at Harpers Ferry.
He brought the Richmond Grays, a beautiful company
and the best-drilled in the state, the Young Guards and
a German company, all under Colonel Wyatt Elliott. At
5 a company from Newton arrived and volunteer com-

panies from Fauquier and Page Counties, who came on
their own account having heard there was fighting here.
That was because a gentleman from the West said there
was an armed force in Ohio getting ready to attack us.
Dispatches from the governor and the marshal of Ohio
confirmed this. Governor Wise reviewed the troops this
evening and while he was doing it the Petersburg Artillery arrived. They only stayed awhile and then went back
to the Ferry. The hotels are all crowded and all vacant
houses are appropriated for barracks and a great many
are quartered on private families. Tonight, just as I had
finished supper, the bell rang and an officer of the Newton
Cavalry presented himself, a friend of mine, and asked me
please to give him supper. He rode all last night and all
today and had nothing to eat but his breakfast. He said
he had gotten places for all his men. We gave him supper
and his room . . .

There were two shows daily on the street. One was
the passage from the jail to the courthouse (old then,
older now and a structure of much dignity) diagonally
opposite. The militia formed a lane through which the
four prisoners—Brown, Stevens, Green, and Coppoc
—were taken, the first two on litters.

The other was less seemly. The Commonwealth's
attorney was Charles Harding, a hopeless drunk. Pre-
siding Judge Richard Parker, whose magnificent handling of an almost impossible judicial duty won him
grudging praise in the North, was afraid to entrust the
prosecution to him, and turned it over to Andrew
Hunter. Thereafter, Harding spent the recesses on
corners, weaving and denouncing practically everybody. When there was talk of turning Stevens over to
the federal government for trial he held forth on the
courthouse steps:

"By God, sir! Wise won't have him and neither will the United States. I know my position. The government'll wait till we get through with them. It can have dead bodies if it likes. By God! I don't owe my office to Wise. I owe it to the voice of the people and I get fifty dollars for trying these cases. That God damned Hunter has honeyfugled me long enough and I mean to take the bit in my teeth. I am going to have the first hanging of these bastards."

Someone who listened to these street-corner orations said, "If you closed your eyes, at first you could imagine you were listening to Patrick Henry, for Harding was an orator. But then he'd mumble and go off into drunken inanities."

The jury was out forty-five minutes. The verdict was guilty. Judge Parker, in a courtroom jammed to the doors, asked Brown if he had anything to say.

The old border soldier arose then. He stood as straight as a youth, all six feet of him. He looked squarely at the bench and uttered one of the great extemporaneous speeches, not to a little courtroom in a sleepy Virginia town, not to the greatest crowd it had ever drawn, but to the world and to history's millenniums:

"I have, may it please the court, a few words to say.

"In the first place, I deny all but what I have all along admitted: of a design on my part to free slaves. I intended certainly to have made a clean thing of that matter, as I did last winter, when I went into Missouri and there took slaves without the snapping of a gun on either side, moving them through the country, and finally leaving them in Canada. I designed to have done the same thing again on a larger scale. That was all I intended. I never did intend murder, or treason, or the destruction of property, or to excite or incite slaves to rebellion, or to make insurrection.

"I have another objection, and that is that it is unjust that I should suffer such a penalty. Had I interfered in the manner which I admit, and which I admit has been fairly proved—for I admire the truthfulness and candor of the greater portion of the witnesses who have testified in the case—had I so interfered in behalf of the rich, the powerful, the intelligent, the so-called great, or in behalf of any of their friends, either father, mother, brother, sister, wife, or children, or any of this class, and suffered and sacrificed what I have in this interference, it would have been all right. Every man in this court would have deemed it an act worthy of reward rather than punishment.

"This court acknowledges, too, I suppose, the validity of the law of God. I see a book kissed, which I suppose to be the Bible, or at least the New Testament, which teaches me that all things whatsoever I would that men should do to me, I should do even so to them. It teaches me, further, to remember them that are in bonds as bound with them. I endeavored to act up to that instruction. I say I am yet too young to understand that God is any respecter of persons. I believe to have interfered as I have done, as I have always freely admitted I have done, in behalf of His despised poor, I did no wrong, but right. Now if it is deemed necessary that I should forfeit my life for the furtherance of the ends of justice, and mingle my blood further with the blood of my children and with the blood of millions in this slave country whose rights are disregarded by wicked, cruel, and unjust enactments, I say, let it be done.

"Let me say one word further. I feel entirely satisfied with the treatment I have received on my trial. Considering all the circumstances, it has been more generous than I expected. But I feel no consciousness of guilt. I have stated that I never had any design against the liberty of any person, nor any disposition to commit treason or incite slaves to rebel or make any general insurrection. I never encouraged any men to do so, but always discouraged any idea of that kind.

"Let me say, also, in regard to the statements made by some of those who were connected with me, I hear it has been stated by some of them that I induced them to join me. But the contrary is true. I do not say this to injure them, but as regretting their weakness. Not one but joined me of his own accord, and the greater part at their own expense. A number of them I never saw, and never had a word of conversation with till the day they came to me, and that was done for the purpose I have stated.

"Now, I have done."

The judge waited a moment. The courtroom was barely breathing. Then he said:

"For the crimes of which you have been convicted I sentence you, John Brown, to be hanged by the neck until dead on Friday, December 2, 1859. The hanging shall be public. I can see no reasonable doubt of your guilt. And may God have mercy on your soul."

9

Five more are to be hanged—Edwin Coppoc, Green, Stevens, Hazlett, Cook—but this is the only one that signifies. December 2 was a cool clear day. Brown wrote one last message to the world, one of his finest, and went out into the bright morning. He looked at the throngs in the streets and the hundreds of smartly caparisoned militiamen and he remarked to his jailer, John Avis, "I had no idea Governor Wise thought my execution so important."

The bystander was looking at the paper the old demon had given him, as though it might burn sulphurous at any moment. It read:

I John Brown am now quite *certain* that the crimes of this *guilty land will* never be purged away; but with Blood. I had *as I now think:* vainly flattered myself that without *very much* bloodshed it might be done.

He wore a black frock coat and black pantaloons. His hat was black and he had white socks under his red carpet slippers. The noose was already around his neck and he had concealed the rope's length in the bosom of the coat. He walked steadily to the wagon for the two-block ride to the field in which the gibbet had been set up. There were nearly four thousand soldiers in the town and hundreds of them, like London bobbies at a coronation, lined each curb to keep everyone out of the roadway.

The press of the North howled and threatened, moralized and wept. The editors did their level damnedest and can be credited with a large assist on the war which resulted. There were some flacks among them; the story of the little nigger baby is as good as anything that ever came out of Paramount's publicity department. As Brown approached his doom, said the fictioneer who wrote it, a Negro mother approached him and he paused to kiss and bless the babe in her arms. Ha! The way they had the town locked up the Virgin herself couldn't have gotten within a block of Brown, except by divine intercession.

Jailer Avis, who had become Brown's good friend and who was willed one of his pistols, asked him if he were afraid.

"It has been characteristic of me from infancy not to suffer from physical fear. I have suffered a thousand times more from bashfulness than from fear." He looked about him. "This *is* a beautiful country. I never had the pleasure of seeing it before."

The field in which he was to be hanged crawled with soldiery like an ancient cheese with maggots. There was history all about the old man. Behind the gallows, at rigid attention, stood the cadets of Virginia Military Academy, spectacularly young in their blue and red uniforms; at their head was the mathematics professor, Thomas J. Jackson, who would stand like a stone wall and then "cross over the river and go into the trees" in a very little time. Captain Turner Ashby, whose dashing gallantry gave him a photo finish with Stuart for the most beautiful cavalryman of the war, rode a snow-white stallion. Lee was back at the Ferry, in command. And in the ranks of the Richmond Grays stood John Wilkes Booth, who had been making the young ladies of the town to swoon by reading Shakespeare to them in the evenings.

The old man scrambled down from the wagon with alacrity when it stopped. No one who saw him die could see the slightest sign of flinching; being Southerners they could, in his last moments, continue to hate him for his principles, but they had to admire him as a man. He said good-by to those nearest him calmly and stood as they tied his arms at the elbows and adjusted the black cap. For twelve mortal minutes they let him stand there, not from cruelty but because some bumbleheaded officer had decided a hollow square would be a nice effect and his kid soldiers didn't know how to arrive at it. Once Avis asked if he would say anything, and Brown replied, "No; just be quick."

Sheriff Brown swung his hatchet. The trap fell.

Actor Booth turned buckskin-white and tried to keep from vomiting on the front of his gorgeous uniform. Idiotically, he asked the man next to him if he had a drink of whiskey.

Jackson told his wife in a letter immediately afterward, "Awful was the thought that in an instant this man might hear the sentence, 'Depart ye wicked, into everlasting fire!' I hope he was ready to go but I fear he wasn't."

An unidentified old Kansan, who had left the state because of the guerrilla war, said to a bystander, "Thank God I've seen him drop. I'm ready to go home to Kansas now."

10

There are always bodies to be disposed of after carnage. In honorable war there is some dignity to it. In treason they become carcasses, to be shoved somewhere out of sight as quickly as possible.

The bodies of Leeman, William Thompson, and Watson Brown had been crammed into barrels by the busy boys from the Winchester Medical College and shipped there as anatomical specimens; many years later Watson's turned up in Indiana and in due course was reinterred at the North Elba farm. Oliver Brown and the six others killed at the Ferry were delivered to one Charles Johnson, who for a fee of $5 wrapped them in their shawls and placed them in two large boxes, which were buried almost at water's edge on the Loudoun side of the Shenandoah. Forty years later they were disinterred and carried to the Adironacks for burial near Brown, Stevens, and Hazlett.

Governor Wise, who had told Mayor Fernando Wood of New York in a letter, "Brown's body shall be delivered to our surgeons, and await the resurrection without a grave in our soil," relented somewhat and agreed that Mrs. Brown might take him home. In the interim an opportunist, Dr. A. E. Peticolas, professor of anatomy at the Medical College of Virginia, wrote this to the governor:

We desire, if Brown and his coadjutors are executed, to add their heads to the collection in our museum. If the transference of the whole bodies will not exceed five dollars each [he wanted bargains, yet!] we should also be glad to have *them*.

Barnum, of course, was not to be left out of all this; his agent had offered Brown $100 for his clothing and pike, to garb and arm a wax figure.

But it cannot be said that Virginia shirked the tidying up any more than it had the harsh work of dispensing justice. The state covered itself with glory throughout: in the fairness of the trial, the fine treatment the men were given in jail, and now in the case of Brown's corpse. Mrs. Brown had come down from New York for a last visit, and had waited in Harpers Ferry, solicitously tended by Hector Tyndale, who will be back in a couple of years to write an ironic postscript made up of the stuff of war.

Brown's wife and the mother of his thirteen children (he had seven by a first wife) was a strong woman. She had to be. Except when he was begetting children, her husband had spent most of his time in wild and remote places, fighting wildly for what was then a remote cause. Now she waited patiently for the special two-car train, with a bodyguard of fifteen civilians, to chug the ten miles from Charlestown. If she heard a lout named H. D. Middlekauff say, at the odor from the coffin, "He was a damn' bad case and they don't keep long," she gave no sign. She thanked Pat Higgins when he helped transship the coffin from the Winchester road to the B. & O.; he remembered her as "a nice little woman." And she carried her mourning well as the cortege went North, through the towns where the bells tolled and the cities where the indignation meetings seethed and into the bleakness of the Adirondacks, where her husband was placed beside a boulder as big and as unyielding as his abolitionist soul.

There were four widows at the graveside . . . men's follies always make widows. There were Mrs. Brown, the wives of Oliver and Watson, and Mrs. William Thompson.

"John Brown's body . . ."

11

There is nothing [the young lady we have met before was to write in a day or two] to interest and amuse us since the soldiers left. Numbers of presents have arrived from the officers of the Richmond, Petersburg and Fincastle companies to their hosts and hostesses. Mrs. Asquith, daughter of the cashier, received a tea service of plate from the Richmond Grays who stayed there. The Richmond men with Mrs. Keyes sent a Sheffield tray and ice pitcher with solid silver goblets. Petersburg Grays sent Mr. Craighill a cheque for $110. The same company sent Jane Beall, sister of the editor, an elegant gold watch and chain. The Fincastle company sent Mrs. Beard a superb silver goblet lined with gold. From Richmond, Mrs. White received a set of plate, coffee pot, tea pot, water jug, cream jug, sugar bowl and slop bowl. Mrs. Rutherford also received an ice-water set. Sallie Brown had sent to her an elegant papier-mâché Chinese cabinet, inlaid with mother-of-pearl beautifully fitted, and one of the Grays who had gone to New York sent Mrs. Brown a gold-lined berry spoon and sugar sifter. Twelve Petersburg Grays sent Mrs. Brown a beautiful solid silver flagon with gold-lined goblets on a large tray, inscribed: "A memento of soldiers' gratitude for woman's welcome, December, 1859."

This, as we all know, was the spirit in which the women of the South approached a war . . . as a thing exciting, like a ball only better, as a time to be so infinitely more important to their men than they could be at any other time.

SIX

Harper's Weekly

1

No sane man would attempt to write anything detailed about the Civil War without a library of evidence to support his slightest claim. The Civil War buffs, those characters who know how many men had dysentery at Cold Harbour and whether Lee ever wore body lice, are so articulate they sometimes seem to outnumber the entire population of the United States. Let the author misplace a comma in the terms of surrender as agreed to at Appomattox and he sets a thousand pairs of eyes ablaze, puts several hundred furious pens to scorching paper.

But as has been said, this book does not pretend to

be a history. It is a memoir. There is no occasion, actually, to be very historical about Harpers Ferry during what my Southern friends insist was the War Between the States. Again, as before, statistics and facts fade into utter insignificance when placed against the tone of the time. Even though you think upon it a great deal, it is hard to believe there was just one community—and that a terribly important one— which was in the theater of war and yet never in the war at all. The Ferry, in the moments it took Lieutenant Roger Jones' men to fire the powder trains and destroy the Works, became disembodied, a nova floating aimlessly in a firmament where all else was plan and intent. A town became a *thing*, a name upon a map, an objective important only because of its physical location and of the railroad that ran through it. Its people became not unlike the eternally neutral Swiss, except that they took a worse beating than the citizens of actively belligerent communities.

No place ever had the cards more carefully stacked against it in a war. It is incredible there could be so many factors to add to the misery of the place. Its internal political sentiment comes first, of course. While it was Southern in sympathy when fully populated, it became indefinite after the younger men, Rebels to their last indignant "Suh!", went rushing off to enlist. The older folk, many of whom had come from the North as artisans to man the armory, remained loyal to the Union but not very vociferously so. They took what came, praying it would be a short war and they would soon be permitted to go back to their jobs of making guns. As victim of the first great devastation, the Ferry remained stunned for a long time, in a state of shock not unlike that after Pearl Harbor. In the midst of what they believed to be peace, the Ferrians saw their greatest institution vanish in a few puffs of smoke, a few globules of flame.

To complicate this dreamlike condition, there was the importance of the Ferry, politically and militarily. The Baltimore & Ohio Railroad, of course, was the big prize. It ran partly through Maryland and then for a long way through Virginia. While Maryland wavered, and while the South believed it would secede, Virginia walked warily where the railroad was concerned. In time, as will be seen, the B. & O. became a Union line, and the South did what it could about that.

When Jackson was first placed in command of the Ferry, he urged Lee to let him fortify Maryland Heights, because without it his position would be untenable. Lee resisted this for a time, fearful that he would so offend the Marylanders they would not come into the Confederacy at all; but Jackson went ahead, finally, placing his artillery on the cliff and manning much of it with Maryland volunteers, thinking thus to appease Baltimore and Annapolis.

Finally, to make the divorcement of Harpers Ferry from all things stable quite complete, there was the feeling in the western counties of Virginia, through which ran the B. & O. The background and the culture of the people there were in no sense Southern, and long before they took action it was a foregone conclusion they would side with the North. And, as it turned out, nothing could save the Ferry from being dragged along with them into the Union.

So, for yet another time, the strange and the unbeautiful are going to happen to our village, adding to the whole emotion we have been absorbing all this time.

2

Captain John D. Imboden was going about his business in Staunton when a Negro boy brought him a telegram, written in that beautiful flowing script which, after speed at receiving, was the great pride of the old telegrapher. It was from Nat Tyler, editor of the Richmond *Enquirer* and read: "Can you come to Richmond at once on military matter of great importance?"

He commanded the Staunton Artillery, one of those quasi-military, quasi-social outfits, but Imboden was a pretty good soldier for all that. He did not waste any time on telegraphic inquiries but went to Richmond. He did not have to go hunting up Tyler to find out the score; he met Henry A. Wise, who had ended his term as governor and was now a Delegate from Princess Anne County and who not only told him the score but briefed him on the other team.

"John," Wise said, "I can't give you the details here in the street. But find all the officers you know and ask them to be at the Exchange Hotel at seven tonight. They're going to be needed—for something big."

Imboden asked no questions. I've often wondered about that, about how military men can be teased

with such exciting hints and salute and go smartly off,
waiting until God (and the general) decide to tell
them the secret; and I've decided it's the masochist
in them. They must like to torment themselves for
hours when often, as in the case of Wise, a simple,
"Hell, no, I won't chase officers—unless you tell me
why" would have gotten a quick answer.

However. Imboden found a number of militia officers, the most notable being Turner Ashby and his
brother Richard, and also Alfred M. Barbour, superintendent of the Harpers Ferry Works. He passed the
word along and, it is to be presumed, spent the afternoon in the hotel bar, being ever so Southern and discussing the action of the Secession Convention, then
sitting. The date, by the way, was April 15, 1861.

Sumter had been fired on five days before and Virginia had wrestled with her conscience every minute
since. The hotheads wanted to secede at once and
march on Washington. The sensible men, like Lee
and Jackson, found themselves fearfully torn. They
were as men told they must decide who should die,
mother or wife. They were married to the Union;
they believed in it; they loved it. But Virginia was
mother. Long before there had been a Union there
had been Virginia. Long before there had been a
New York, to amount to anything, there had been a
Williamsburg, to amount to everything. The statesmen Virginia had—and she was always plentifully
supplied—tried in the convention to hammer out a
solution that would do two things: permit the Cot-
ton and Gulf States, if they chose, to form their own
country, and do it without war.

When they met at seven, Wise went directly to the point. He proposed the immediate seizure of Harpers Ferry. When the protestants spoke of this as an action against the United States he replied, "By the time you get your troops there, ready for action, Virginia will be out of the Union."

We can pause a moment and look at that. Wise announced the seizure to the convention on the 17th— eighteen months to the day from the time old Brown had attacked, and Wise had denounced the abolitionists as "murderers, traitors, insurrectionists," and had pledged them no mercy as "wanton, unprovoked felons." Now he was heading up a movement identical with Brown's; his promise to wait for a vote on secession was a politician's, for he knew well that all Virginia needed was a decisive act. By providing it in the capture of Harpers Ferry he would assure the secession vote. His reasoning was identical with that of Brown, who was so sure a decisive act would arouse the slaves in such a way as to free them without full-scale war.

Imboden and the others bought the idea, without haggling. They were told off to alert troops along the way and arrange trains to carry them. Imboden went to call on Governor Letcher, who received him in a nightshirt hours after midnight, and who said he would authorize nothing until secession had been voted, but would authorize anything then. The wires to the soldiers went out on the 16th, ordering them to stand by in their armories for a movement to seize the Portsmouth Navy Yard. There were leaks in the telegraph, that they knew, and there were other

leaks. On the train carrying the Richmond con-
tingent North a traveler overheard Barbour being
indiscreet and wrote a dispatch to President Lincoln,
but the darky who took his dollar to send it kept the
dollar and gave the message to Imboden.

Captain Charles Dimmock, West Pointer, North-
erner by birth and Southerner by sympathy, was in
command of the Richmond armory. He gave Imboden whatever munitions he needed. The advance
guard set out at daybreak April 17, with no action
as yet taken on secession. But by noon the convention
had been treated to some pyrotechnics by Wise. He
entered the chamber late and before he sat down he
placed a large horse pistol on his desk. Then, clearing
his throat, he tuned up to full volume and let them
have it: "Gentlemen, at this moment a force is on its
way to capture Harpers Ferry in the glorious name
of Virginia and the Confederate States of America!
There will be a fight or a footrace between the volunteers of Virginia and the federal troops before the
sun sets this day!"

Someone protested, "It's war!" and Wise answered
somewhat in the vein of his speeches throughout that
year:

"Very well, it's war. We can fight them. Get a
spear, a lance. Take a lesson from old John Brown.
Manufacture your blades from old iron, even though it
be the tires of your cart wheels.

"Your true-blooded Yankee, suhs, will never stand
still in the presence of cold steel!"

So, because that sort of thing was as effective then
as it is now, they voted Virginia out of the Union. Im-

boden, riding north to Staunton, still did not know
what his orders would be and worried. But at the station he was reassured. Thousands of people had
streamed in from all over Augusta County. His artillery was lined up, as brightly uniformed as the soldiers of a Viennese operetta, and beside it the West
Augusta Guards, finest company in the Valley. Major General Kenton Harper, veteran of the Mexican
war, was on hand, with instructions from Governor
Letcher to take charge.

They went on by train at sundown. At Charlottes-
ville they picked up the Monticello Guards; at Culpeper a rifle company came aboard. At Manassas
Junction came word that Turner Ashby's cavalry
would go ahead and rendezvous with the foot soldiers
near the Ferry.

Trains were impressed for the trip to Strasburg, and Imboden was placed in charge of the first.
A few miles out of Manassas it began to crawl, unaccountably. Then the train came to a dead standstill
on a very slight grade. Imboden went ahead and
found the engineer to be a dirty Yankee, who had de-
liberately let his fire die down. The Virginian
climbed into the cab, let the engineer have a good
look at his cocked revolver, and pointed out that when
lead enters the human body through the skin death
quite often results. "We made a good forty miles an
hour then," said Imboden, "with the aid of dry wood
and that Navy revolver."

At Strasburg they went looking for horses. A good
many of the farmers they approached were more interested in the spring plowing than in a thing called

secession, so the teams had to be taken by force. There was a silly civilian threat of indictment for horse stealing by the next grand jury, but none of the soldiers paid much attention to that. They reached Winchester at nightfall and were received very coldly; the people of the "Bandy Ball of the South" could not know that before 1865 they would learn how to live with war, in misery and a finer pride than they themselves believed they had.

Harper had moved his infantry up to Charlestown and the artillery followed. The guns were unloaded at Halltown, to be run forward by hand to Bolivar for a possible shelling of the exposed buildings beneath.

Meanwhile, Superintendent Barbour had returned to the Works. He called in Lieutenant Jones, whose command of forty-two soldiers had been sent down from Carlisle Barracks in answer to Barbour's own plea the preceding January for protection. Barbour told the lieutenant what the convention had decided, said he was throwing in with the Confederacy, and waited. Jones dead-panned it. He replied that he was an officer of the United States Army and would take orders from his superiors in Washington.

Barbour then addressed the workmen, most of them from the North, and offered them securities and high wages if they would stay on and make guns for the Confederacy. They had pans as dead as Jones'.

Sometime during the 17th, Jones wired headquarters saying he could not possibly hold the Works unless men "and by the thousands are sent to support me." Washington replied that the nearest reinforce-

ment, a thousand Massachusetts volunteers then in
the capital, could not reach the Ferry in time to prevent any action, and told the lieutenant to blow up
the Works and withdraw if he were attacked.

Powder trains were laid through all the buildings
and in the Hall Rifle Factory on Virginius Island.
The lieutenant and his forty-two soldiers waited.
Southern sympathizers among the workmen crept
through the armory, throwing water on such powder
trains as were not guarded. Just before dawn Jones
heard firing on Bolivar Heights. He also studied, in
his mind, the sheaf of whispered messages the citizens had given him, of a great horde complete with
cannon closing in on the Ferry. He must have been
quite a boy, this Roger Jones. He waited until there
could be no doubt. Then he ordered the trains
lighted. He left a rear guard of four men, all of whom
escaped by swimming the river, and marched his
thirty-eight others across the bridge as though he
were on parade. As his feet touched Maryland soil he
could hear the enraged howls of the rebels, pouring
down the hill from Bolivar into the dazzling floodlight
thrown by the blazing Works.

The fires were put out but not until all but a thousand or so of the twenty thousand guns were destroyed.
The tools and machinery in the armory were blackened but reparable, and were moved piecemeal into
factories farther south. The Hall Works was virtually
picked up bodily and, biblically, taken on a flight
into Egypt—Egypt, North Carolina, to be exact.

By the end of the week there were 1,300 Virginia
militiamen in the town. A major general commanded

and there were three brigadiers. The staffs of these, and the staffs of the staffs, made for a hell of a lot of military pomp. "Every afternoon the official display of fuss and feathers would have done credit to the Champs-Élysées," said an unromantic type who watched it all.

Major General Harper decided to prevent any troop movement on the Baltimore & Ohio. He had cannon placed to command the tracks and stationed pickets far up the line. The first prisoner he took was by accident; a nervous vedette thought he saw some soldiers and fired, and before the train could be stopped every picket was blazing away at it. Being indifferent shots, no damage was done. The officer in charge went aboard and demanded that the conductor turn over the Yankees he was carrying. The conductor shifted his cud. "Only military I got aboard, bub," he said easily, "is up in the baggage car, asleep on mail sacks."

The Virginian, deploring the conductor's English, went forward, where he found the English to be precisely right. Old Brigadier General W. S. Harney lay on the sacks, sleeping all curled up like a fetus, and when they woke him up he explained he was on his way to Washington to resign his commission and go to Europe. He wanted no part of a fratricidal war, but he did not at all mind being one of its first prisoners. They made a big fuss over the old man, with generals and staff officers escorting him wherever he went, and in a few days sent him to Richmond, which in turn sent him on to Washington.

Then, on April 27, the bubble burst for the toy

soldiers. Lee took over as commander-in-chief and every militia officer above the rank of captain was busted. To take command of Harpers Ferry came Thomas J. Jackson, a dreamy mathematics professor at V.M.I., but the strongest right arm any commanding general ever had.

With Jackson came discipline and austerity. And some rather astonishing victories.

3

Now you remember what Steinbeck said, that a town has a nervous system and a head and shoulders and feet. All of a sudden Harpers Ferry had no head. It had all the rest, but it was in the most literal sense a decapitated community. It had a nervous system and still has. It had shoulders and it had feet, too much of both to be pleasing to strangers who kept making entrances and exits and carrying on in them like the loudest Shakespearean actor ever born.

At this point, the Ferry began to know what it was like to be a *thing*. It was a nuisance but a necessary one. It was like, say, the meek little man just before Christmas, who tries clumsily to get through a revolving door with all his packages and accomplishes nothing but to get buffeted about and to irritate more efficient people. Or it was like the small boy who has managed to slither through the police line and now seems, to the busy firemen at a threealarmer, to be not one boy under foot but an antlike army of small boys.

The war's beginnings were in the strictest *Gone with the Wind* tradition, so we shall do no more than sample them anecdotally and then get on with it.

The first thing to collapse was the monetary system. Even before Jackson took over, General Harper (no relation to Robert, by the way) tried to buy stores for his troops and complained to Richmond, "Even Virginia money will procure nothing, except at an enormous discount, at the stores here."

The youth rushed to enlist in the Southern forces. Henry Kyd Douglass III, of Shepherdstown (he who had unwittingly helped Brown unload his "machinery") wrote in his diary:

> Society was plentiful, for the ranks were filled with the best blood of Virginia; all its classes were there. Mothers and sisters and dear girls came constantly to the Ferry and there was little difficulty in seeing them. Nothing was serious yet. George Flagg, crossing the parade ground was joshed and he said to his tormentors, "These buckets aren't filled with slops. They're full of patriotism."

And then Douglass, later to be Jackson's aide, was sent to burn the highway bridge at Shepherdstown. He stood and watched. "When in the glare of the glowing timbers I saw the windows of my home on the hill beyond the river and knew my father was a stockholder in the property I was helping to destroy, I realized that war had begun."

Over the years the churches became hospitals, those that were undamaged, and the Harper grave-

yard held out its arms to many alien men. The first of
these was a boy from the Fifteenth Pennsylvania,
who died of typhoid. He was given a fine funeral,
with six comrades carrying his coffin and others standing at present arms, with muffled drums, with a volley
over the grave.

It was thus that we buried the strange soldier [wrote
Alonzo Hall Quint, chaplain of the Second Massachu-
setts]. He had no friend who knew him here. No kindred
wept by the side of the grave. His bed was made alone,
in a deserted graveyard, on the bold cliff that overlooked
the two rivers united in the mighty stream that pours its
affluence into the Atlantic. The soldiers subdued their
roughness and laid him down tenderly. The frequent oath
was unheard. The solemn silence was scarcely broken by
the low words of command. When the sharp volley
echoed up and down the valleys, the shadows had already
fallen on the lordly rivers; but the gorgeous evening sun-
light was richly clothing the dark forest greens of both
Maryland and Virginia, towering over us. His grave was
out in a hard and rocky soil, but out of that soil the ever-
green was thriving and the wild flowers perfumed the
air . . . And soon we struck our tents and forded the
dark and foaming river which separated the rebel from
the loyal state.
  He had forded a darker and rougher river.

Today's mecca for the Kodak brigade is Jefferson's Rock. But the soldiers of the Civil War didn't
give a damn about Jefferson; Northerners and Southerners alike wanted to see what was to be seen in connection with old Brown. They examined the engine
house, with the loopholes still where stuttering Phil
Luckum had cut them, and sent home splinters and

bits of brick as souvenirs. They traipsed out to visit
the Kennedy farm, and to examine Lind Currie's
schoolhouse. One Massachusetts private, after a
glance at the mud-chinked logs, said, "Why, hell,
these people ain't even civilized. Teach kids in that!
Why, hell, our pigs in Massachusetts have better
houses than that."

It was very hard, in the Ferry, to separate people
from a cause. There was the little boy who, late in
1861, became very fond of a Yankee captain. His wid-
owed mother was fond of the captain, too, apparently, but she had to try and conceal it. The boy got
permission to look at the captain's pistol and turned.
"You may look at it, Mother. But"—the awakening
male—"be careful you don't shoot Captain Maxwell."

She smiled down at him. "Captain Maxwell's a
Yankee—don't you think he *ought* to be shot?"

The boy dug a toe in the dirt, looked from
his mother to the captain, answered as a true Virginian, "Oh, all right. Go ahead and shoot him."

(From over near Shepherdstown came the standard story of the boy in blue who cried "Halt!" to the
boy in gray who refused to halt and was killed by
the boy in blue who learned then that the boy in gray
was his brother. This one was repeated so many
times it would appear that the Union and Confederate armies were exactly evenly divided, brother
against brother all the way down the line.)

It's amusing to look at the anecdotes today. But
they couldn't have been anecdotes then. They could
only have been life's tears, which in retrospect become history's wisecracks.

4

Away back in the previous act we met a spear-carrier named Jackson, who stood with his cadets at the Brown execution. He re-enters now, as the one bright star of the Ferry's wartime drama. They summoned him from his classes at Lexington and he came in his dingy blue professor's uniform, Major Thomas J. Jackson then. They put him in the topographical department, which is par for stupidity's course in any army, and he was miserable there, being a rotten draftsman. Then headquarters got some reports about the peacocks supposed to be defending Harpers Ferry and sent him there to take command.

Jackson, you might say, crept into town. He was the most unobtrusive of men, mounted on a cob named Old Sorrel and always with his ancient cadet cap pulled down over his dark expressionless eyes. He took a small room in the Wager House, sharing it with his adjutant, and it was as monastic as he liked: two cots, two straight chairs, and a big deal table for the spreading of maps. He issued orders, about discipline mostly, telegraphic in their brevity. He would have none of the posing on the streets and this sent the deposed staff officers bustling off to Richmond, with their indignation preceding them like the blasts of a streamliner's horn. This Jackson, they said, is trying to make a harsh business out of war, when we

all know it's a gallant kind of lark and we can whip
the Yankees any Wednesday (the way we did the Jap-
anese fleet in 1941).

But whatever the officers thought, the 4,500 men
Jackson commanded learned a lesson. He was so much
the embodiment of duty they could not question his
honesty and the more they watched him—with the
patience of a plaster saint for those who tried and the
wrath of the Old Testament Jehovah for those who
shirked—the more they came to know that this was
a grim dedication they had assumed and its end could
be only suffering and dirty death. They groused at
the seven daily hours of drill, but they obeyed and in
time began to feel an alien pride that they knew one
foot from the other. Presently "Beauty" Stuart turned
up, "as boisterous as March, as fresh as May," and his
ineffable gustiness infected them all; they liked his
gaudy sashes and they loved to march with him because he led them in roaring masculine songs at the
head of the column.

For a few weeks there was nothing much to do except try to whip raw recruits into the semblance of
soldiers and to watch the enemy across the Potomac.
But Jackson had a fine thinking machine back of
the whiskers and the steady eyes. Hadn't he studied,
in the evenings at Lexington, by sitting upright
in a chair facing the wall and just *thinking* about tomorrow's mathematical problems? He listened to the
trains, day and night, rumbling over the long covered bridge. The B. & O. was doubletracked from
Point of Rocks to Cherry Run, some thirty-two miles,
and it moved a lot of traffic in every twenty-four

hours, coal for the seaboard mostly. Stonewall did not like those trains. Presently, he had devised a stratagem and he wrote one of his succinct orders, to Robert Garrett, president of the B. & O.

Garrett was a tycoon, a dictator, a fatso, so much so his system was called "Garrett's Railroad." The history of the road, by Edward Hungerford, makes him look sickeningly like a combination of God the Father, Socrates, and the man who discovered the principle of the wheel. But he was just an ordinary executive, of the sort who gains fame by raising hell with some poor devil for being sixty seconds late in ringing a train's starting bell, or for burning too much gas in Baltimore's Camden Station. He was a great railroader, for all that he was a spoiled brat given to roarings when he didn't get his way, and he made his line perform miracles all through the war. And now he was a man much confused. His world was Baltimore, where the railroad had been born, and in the beginning Maryland didn't know whether it was Union or Confederate. (In a sense, to digress, it still doesn't; your third- or fourth-generation Marylander is likely to be so disgustingly Southern as to suggest a parody.) Garrett began by being Christlike about it all, referring to the seceded states as "our Southern friends." Then, when he saw that he would have to do with Union butter for the B. & O.'s bread, it became "our misguided Southern friends." Then when they began to interfere with train movement, it was "those Rebels" and finally, when they tore up the railroad every hour on the hour, it was "those God damned Rebel bastards," or an equivalent.

And there we have a pretty picture. The shabby professor-in-arms sends a peremptory note to the Leader of Men who is to be all but deified by his biographer. But the professor has guns and the tycoon has only a railroad he must keep operating, and again the fact that we live in a world of compromise is crashingly demonstrated.

Stonewall informed the president that the noise of his trains at night "disturbs the repose of my men and must cease." Garrett bowed and started running trains only in daylight hours, crowding both tracks to capacity. Jackson waited a little and then sent word that nobody could hear himself think, with all that racket and thereafter Mr. Garrett would kindly make tonnage movements only between the hours of 11 A.M. and 1 P.M. Garrett again obeyed, and the trains roared through the Ferry like elephants that had stampeded but forgotten to drop one another's tails.

Imboden was sent to Point of Rocks about this time, on a report that General B. F. ("Beast") Butler was at Relay House, a little farther east, and might be expected to try some tricks at any moment. Imboden stayed awake nights and slept by day to be ready for anything, and on a drowsy Sunday afternoon received the order toward which Jackson had been working since he sent Garrett the first ultimatum.

"Promptly at eleven o'clock, stop all east-bound rail traffic but permit west-bound proceed."

To Kenton Harper, now a regular colonel, at Martinsburg, went a similar order, which would let the east-bound trains run and hold the west-bound. In an hour, Jackson had tidily bottled up fifty-six locomotives and more than three hundred cars. The very light engines, which would weigh not much more than a six-horse Conestoga, went over the Winchester line, and then, on great wagons, to Strasburg. The others were run back to Martinsburg. The little ones, by the way, did yeoman service just before the First Bull Run, hauling in the troops the Confederacy needed for its first great victory.

Somewhere along here Lee wondered if this professor was enough of a soldier to be in charge of the Ferry and decided not. General Joe Johnston was ordered to take command. Johnston fell back to Winchester, presently, and left Jackson with the job of destroying "*all* the railroad property at Martinsburg." With an obedience the Wheeling *Intelligencer* called "almost as villainous as the crime of murder" Jackson burned the roundhouses, hundreds of loaded three-pot coal cars, and forty-two locomotives. Writing sorrowfully to his wife, he said of this: "If the cost of the property could have been disseminating the gospel of the Prince of Peace, how much good might have been expended!" But for all his sorrow he believed in orders and obeyed them to the letter. The coal cars glowed for days. Now there isn't much to burn on a locomotive, and as Jackson regarded them a wonderful idea grew in his mind. The Confederacy needed those engines. Why not get them for the South?

There was only one way, an impossible way, to do it—over the turnpike. He called one Hugh Longust, a veteran railroader from Richmond. Longust took a look and said, "If you can give us the teams to haul 'em, we'll get 'em to Strasburg."

Longust put together a crew of about forty men, with ten expert machinists as its nucleus. Valley farmers brought up forty of their best horses. Harness makers put together record-breaking traces and smith-forged chains. Longust and his gang picked a huge wood-burner, begrimed from the fire, and lifted it on jacks. Then they stripped it of everything they could—rods, pistons, bell, valves, and all the other removable parts. They swung it at right angles to the track and in place of the pilot truck put a wooden dolly, with wide, iron-tired wheels. The drivers, except for the two that had no flanges, were removed.

This done the horses were hitched, four abreast, ten teams deep. A crackling of whipfire ran down the long line. The traces gave off sounds of leather in labor, the long chain, attached to single, double, and "fou'ble" whiffletrees, went taut, and the unhappy engine, not only denuded but now stripped of the dignity of its mission in life, lurched drunkenly off down the pike. The teams filled the roadway solidly. For all of Mr. McAdam's ingenuity, his roads made dust and the horses stirred up an atomic cloud of it. Now and again even forty horses couldn't compete with the grade, and then the men moved in—men recruited anywhere, up to three hundred of them, to grab long ropes and dig into it, noses almost on the paving, like coolies pulling boats up the Whangpoo. On the level sometimes the road would crack under the great weight and the mechanics, following like mourners after a hearse, would rush in with their skills and their big jacks and somehow get the monster back onto solidity again.

This went on for weeks, in the summer of '61, until fourteen of the B. & O.'s best hogs had been hauled to Strasburg. A schedule came into being and the trip became a three-day job: one to Winchester, two more to railhead at Strasburg. The only interruption countenanced was Yankee attack: the snipers would come up in the underbrush and let fly, now and then, and everything living would flee for a time, leaving the engine standing grotesquely, like a fat woman surprised at her bath, in the middle of the pike.

Much of this campaigning was roughly masculine. The language blistered the moon, when they hauled and tugged through the soft Southern nights. But there was still a meed of chivalry about, even among the stinking sleepless men who moved their steel mountains as much by power of will as by physical strength. The handsomest of the engines was earmarked for the shops in Richmond. There it was given a fine walnut cab and brass fittings that would take a fine polish and other ornamentation befitting it to be the *Lady Davis*, in honor of the Confederacy's only First Lady.

Then came Second Bull Run and the Rebels quit Manassas and no more locomotives could go via Strasburg. But there was one brute they needed, a big freight-hauling camel-back. The only possibility was to take to the road again and travel the hundred miles down valley from Strasburg to Staunton. They did it in four days, God knows how. It was all new territory for highway movement of locomotives, and crews had to go ahead to test the bridges and strengthen them where they needed it. The grades were tougher and spots had to be selected for block-and-tackle. But on the evening of the fourth day, with the populace lining the sidewalks as though the circus had come to town, the 199 staggered down Staunton's main street. With all its furbelows missing and its step ever so uncertain, it looked like a dowager caught drunk and half undressed.

By and large, the war gave the B. & O. hell at Harpers Ferry. The bridge was destroyed and rebuilt no fewer than nine times. After Antietam construction crews had to spend their mornings clearing away the bodies of horses and men around the pilings before they could be at their work.

MOSBY

John Moseby was around, ubiquitously around, like the mosquito in the dark room which vanishes when you turn on the light. He tore up the roadbed so many times his raiders became experts at what to do about it. They would make a great bonfire of the sleepers and then heat the rails cherry red. Yelling and singing, they would carry the rails in tongs to big trees and wrap them around and around, so that when they cooled nothing but a furnace could have freed them. They held up the trains, Wild West fashion, and took the railroad's money and that of the Yankees aboard; if a passenger could prove he was a true son of the South his poke was safe. The biggest haul of the lot came in 1854, when Moseby slipped through the Union lines, stuck up the westbound express seven miles from Harpers Ferry, and found two Union paymasters aboard with $173,000. This would surely bring high pursuit, Moseby decided, so to create a diversion and delay the alarm as long as possible he

1864

ordered the train burned and the locomotive's boiler
blown up. There was a car of German immigrants
going West and they declined to budge; Moseby
handed some of his men a bundle of New York *Her-
alds* and said, "Here. Scatter these in the aisle and
drop a match. If the damned Dutchmen won't move
we'll use this sheet to move them—it's all it's good
for."

David Lee, chief of maintenance of way in the Harpers Ferry sector (the most exasperating job, it could
be, in all the war) came around a curve one afternoon on a handcar. There was Moseby smoking a
pipe and there were his boys merrily ripping up the
line. Lee had known Moseby in a happier time. He
hopped off the handcar and strode up to the raider.

"For Christ's sweet sake, John, will you fellows
stop? They're drafting all my men and how the hell
am I going to keep a railroad running with you fellows playing tricks all the time!"

Moseby looked at him indulgently. "Hello, Davey."
He turned to his men, who had paused to listen. "All
right, boys. Put the rails back." Then, to Lee, "Just
this one time, Davey, as a personal favor. We've got a
war to fight."

But like all the rest of it, this was nipping at the
flanks of the dinosaur. The Union couldn't be stopped
and the Baltimore & Ohio, the biggest system of its
day, couldn't be stopped either. After Chickamauga,
with Rosecrans licking his wounds in Chattanooga
and yelling for reinforcements, Garrett and Edwin M.
Stanton, Secretary of War, collaborated on the first
great troop movement by rail in history. An endless

stream of trains was sent west with soldiers riding
in everything from gondolas to Garrett's private car,
and in nine incredible days twenty thousand men,
with their wagons and their mules and the artillery,
were carried from the Potomac to Tennessee. Field
kitchens were spotted along the rights-of-way the
railroads used and the men ate hot meals regularly
en route.

With this sort of thing happening, it is small wonder
indeed that the western part of Virginia decided to
break away and become a state on its own. It was to
have been called Kanawha but the convention finally
settled for West Virginia.

5

Away back there (remember?) the Tidewater was
the gentry and the people of the West merely worked
hard and smelled bad. For this the descendants of the
gents in the powdered wigs and the satin breeches began now, at the very outbreak of the war, to reap their
own particular whirlwind.

For generations the people of the Western Reserve
had chafed that they were not among the bright lights
in the East. They could not be and knew it. Had they
remained nearer the seaboard they never could have
kept up with the aristocratic Joneses. All they had
with which to make a life were courage and brawn
and the ability to get by on sowbelly and pone. They

might have borne this Providential inequity with more grace had not the planters, who dominated first the House of Burgesses and then the legislature, been the greedy bastards their like usually are. The taxes were onerous and worse, because the Easterners had seen to it that there was no tax on slaves under twelve and much of their wealth came from the scientific breeding of Negroes for sale. The East got railroads and canals out of the tax money, and the West was lucky to get a two-rut road now and then.

Even after the war began, the East continued its affected, supercilious superiority over the "peasants of the West." So when the secession was voted, the wise heads among the peasantry decided to resist it; they did not know what the Union would do for portions of states that remained loyal, but they reasoned it surely could do no less than their brethren had throughout all the past. A series of meetings was held in various spots, their best parallel being those just before the French revolution. Morgantown took the first of many votes; on April 17, 1861, it resolved to support the Union whatever came. The citizenry was armed with several hundred rifles, thoughtfully sent to them by Governor Wise after the Harpers Ferry raid. For a time there was anarchy in the western counties, orderly anarchy. Road barricades were set up and no commerce helpful to Virginia was permitted. Strangers were either turned back or taken through the territory under armed guard. Order was as rigidly maintained as it had been in the late days of the California Vigilantes; the opportunists who tried to move in for the fast buck were paid off in the double whammy of the day. The councils continued, in mountain hideaways and other remote places, with the delegates debating whilst leaning negligently on their fowling pieces. When the formal convention of secession from a seceded state was set for Wheeling in June of 1861, there was a full roster of delegates— save from Jefferson County, that nova of the war, which was still being kicked around in front of the revolving door.

Jefferson was not admitted until November, 1863, after some of the shiftiest politicking since Caesar. The voice of the people was permitted to be expressed, but under direction of the Union military commandant. Only two voting precincts were opened in the county, at Shepherdstown and Harpers Ferry. The notice of the election, signed by the military, carried the admonition: "Citizens are warned on this day to stay within their own houses," presumably after they had run as fast as they could all the way to the polls and back. It made little difference. There were no Southern sympathizers left to vote; they were all with the Confederate armies. Only the old folks turned out and how they marked the ballots will never definitely be known. It's a cinch these results, as officially announced, are more fiction than real balloting: Shepherdstown, 196 for separation from Virginia, one against; Harpers Ferry, fifty-two for, one against. (This was called by the Union officers "a full and free expression of the people"; 1,800 had voted in 1860. Q.E.D.)

It was terribly important to the new state of West Virginia that nothing go wrong in this plebiscite, because Jefferson County had the Baltimore & Ohio, and that was the only means of transport to the East. If Jefferson voted to remain with Virginia, and the South won the war, there was no telling what reprisals would be taken against West Virginia, since the B. & O.'s most important link ran through the Old Dominion. Too, if the railroad county was not included, West Virginia might not enjoy the support of the Maryland delegates when Congress took up the enabling act. Then, as now, the railroad was a powerful lobbyist.

"No, sirs," a leader of the convention, Chapman J. Stuart, asked, "unless we have control of this road, what is to become of us? Do you not see? The eastern portion of our state has always been disposed to unfriendly legislation toward us; and now when this excitement is up and we are forming a new state —I appeal to the members of this convention: what do they think will be the legislation of eastern Virginia toward this great improvement, to which every vital interest we have is second?"

Someone pointed out that Jefferson and Berkeley counties had always been proslavery and secessionist. Peter J. Van Winkle, another godfather of the new state, remarked, "That objection, however formidable it may have appeared in the beginning, vanishes and becomes nothing when compared to the material advantage of having a trunk railroad to serve the state." He paused and added, "And if those counties don't vote to come in, I say let's bring them in with the rifle!"

So it was done. A new state was born. And Harpers

Ferry was more the orphan than it had ever been. Well enough for the unreconstructed to insist that their mail be addressed to Harpers Ferry, "in the Western Portion of Virginia," as some were still doing only a few years ago; they were Yankees by fiat and they had to take it, like it or not.

6

Other ravaged cities had a little time before the war swept over them. But not the Ferry. It was plunged into war without notice, dunked as thoroughly and swiftly as a total-immersion Baptist. All business stopped when the Works had been destroyed, except for the the operations of A. H. Herr's big flour mill on Virginius Island. The women baked pies for the soldiers and the men smuggled whiskey to them. Aside from that, the average Ferrian walked about in the streets with a "Wha' hoppen?" expression perpetually on his face.

The first official skirmish involving the village occurred on July 4, 1861, and carried with it that touch of irony which is so persistent in the Ferry's annals. Union snipers fired across the Potomac, wounding one civilian and killing another. The latter, F. A. Roeder, fell almost where Hayward Shepherd had—and, like Shepherd, Roeder was a strong supporter of the very cause which slew him.

The soldiers, Union and Confederate alike, were

not disciplined. They took what they wanted. Their officers commandeered the churches, only the Catholic escaping damage. The Presbyterian suffered the greatest sacrilege, its meeting floor being turned into a guardhouse and its basement into a stable. When Jackson came along to occupy in 1862, he had with him Captain W. H. Pendleton's Stockbridge Artillery. Pendleton had been rector at Lexington and his men insisted he use a pulpit as his private chamber; they made a barracks of the rest of a church and, to signify connection, named their four guns Matthew, Mark, Luke, and John.

The Union forces moved in July 18, 1861, and the townsfolk found them even greater thieves than the rebels. It was a comment of the time that "These cannot be ninety-day enlistees; nobody could develop such a capacity for larceny in so short a time."

Colonel Turner Ashby, the flamboyant cavalryman, killed the Ferry's last industry. And Colonel John W. Geary, for the Union, completed the destruction of the town. These, excepting the Jackson capture of the place in 1862, could be called the two great actions of the war.

Ashby was told by a spy that Herr had offered his supply of flour to the Federal forces if they would come and get it. He marched on the town midway in the movement. "The battle of Bolivar Heights" which followed saw thirteen casualties on either side, but Ashby managed to get to Virginius Island and destroy the Herr mill.

Geary, enraged at the death of a favorite scout, sent a force to burn the balance of the waterfront build-

ings—the station and Wager House, a warehouse, water tower, and several dwellings. And in charge of
these men was Major Hector Tyndale . . . and what
must he have thought, as he stood off and watched the
torch applied?

He must have vividly have recalled the night less
than two years before, when he had waited outside the
Charlestown jail for Mrs. Brown to have her last contained visit with the man they would hang tomorrow.
He had to remember his efforts to be kind to her, to
reach wordless in a sharing of her quiet misery. He
had to look about him and tie together that night with
this; that first mad act from which came this endless
series of mad acts.

All the time, of course, the raiders were busy around
and about our village. Moseby had a lesser-known
counterpart in Samuel G. Means, whose Loudoun
Rangers were called soldiers by the Union and brigands by the South. John Moberly and "French Bill"
Loge were brigands in fact, and when at last Loge
was captured Phil Sheridan's instruction as to him
read: "When you have fully ascertained that you have
French Bill as your prisoner take him out and hang
him."

Moberly, for whom a reward was posted after his
men had murdered a surgeon of the Sixth Pennsylvania Cavalry, was captured. The rope broke when
they tried to hang him and another surgeon, remembering his brother, finished the job with a knife.

By the time the Stonewall Brigade fell upon the
Ferry, a regular routine had been established. The
people ebbed and flowed like an irregular tide, gov-

erned by the insane moon of war. A rumor that the place was about to change hands sent those who could across the Potomac to Frederick, where "Uncle Leilic's" Hotel was the gathering place; there they would stay until it became safe to return.

The astonishing thing about the American people is that in their direst times there is always a wit to put a label on adversity.

The people adopted the word for these hegiras chosen by the wit and thereafter a trip to Frederick became one of the "Skedaddles."

7

Lee had gone into Pennsylvania with a puny sort of force, fifty thousand men. McClellan was stronger and fresher, but Lee was unworried; he had the brains and his men had the spirit. The Rebel ladies of Frederick, sufficiently in the Barbara Frietchie tradition to make that anecdote fairly palatable, called the Confederates "our dirty darlings" and pressed pies upon them as they marched. Dirty darlings they were. They straggled through the towns, not trying to march, with brimless hats and rope for belts and moccasins they'd made themselves for boots. They carried what they owned, most of them, in liberated Union haversacks. They were scarecrows, so lousy they scratched more than they marched.

At Frederick Lee pondered. There were some fifteen thousand Federals at his back, the bulk in Harpers Ferry. He made a daring decision—to split his army almost evenly and send Jackson back to take the Potomac. As it proved, he guessed right. He knew McClellan of old and McClellan was a man who looked several times before he wondered if it would be wise to leap. Even then he often stayed right where he was. When the celebrated "Lost Order"—Lee's detailed instructions for the maneuvering around Sharpsburg during the Antietam campaign, which was found on a Frederick street wrapped around three cigars—fell into his hands he still procrastinated, and Antietam, which should have been a full rout for the Confederates, is scored by most students of tactics as a stalemate.

Jackson moved artillery to the Heights overlooking the Ferry. Below, Colonel Miles, in command of 12,520 men, sent a frantic message to McClellan for support, instructing his courier to "relay this information to someone who may have heard of the United States Army, or any general of the United States Army, or anybody that knows anything about the United States Army." The messenger got through, which was more than any of the three McClellan sent back, each with instructions to Miles to "hold at all costs," could do.

Little damage was done the town—not that there was a hell of a lot left to damage—by Jackson's bombardment. His main target was the Union line on Bolivar Heights, for one thing, and for another the Rebel ammo was faulty, most of it bursting short or just fizzing out. Miles saw no choice but to surrender and he did so seconds before a mortal bullet hit him, thus providing the Federal investigators with a custom-made scapegoat. Jackson moved in, taking his wounded up to the Catholic Church (and giving to the hand-hewn stairway the name it has today, "The Bloody Steps"). He secured his prisoners and arranged for the transport of thirteen thousand small arms and several hundred wagon loads of matériel, excepting the food and clothing he immediately passed out to his hungry legion.

That Jackson. A Presbyterian, soul-bound to duty at whatever cost, and still an occasional softie. He could listen to the plea of a minister for the life of a soldier convicted of talking roughly to women after breaking into a house, agree to commune with God, and next morning order the soldier shot. Or he could interrupt the important work of viewing enemy gun emplacements through his glasses to heed the request of a B. & O. section foreman's wife that he bless her baby, taking the infant into his arms as he sat Old Sorrel. He could blush and stammer when the ladies of Martinsburg invaded his billet, collectively offering him their all, and patiently write his name in the autograph books they shoved at him; and, had it not been thinning, perhaps he might have given them locks of his hair to go with the buttons they snipped off his coat. He could even perform, in another place and in a slightly different way, in that white-plume fashion Whittier credited him with in the Frietchie myth. At Middletown, as he marched toward the Ferry, two young ladies rushed to the curb. They wore red-white-and-blue hair ribbons and giggled madly as they waved little American flags in Stonewall's face. He took off

his cap and bowed to them; he murmured to an aide,
"We evidently do not have many friends here."

He was, to use a trite phrase, a legend in his lifetime.
When the Ferry fell to him, his fame was so great the
Union prisoners lined the curb to watch him march
in. Many uncovered and Jackson returned all salutes
with grave military courtesy. One young Yankee
waited until he was abreast and then said, so the general could hear him:

"Boys, he don't look like much—but if we'd had him
we damn' well wouldn't be in this mess now."

The Confederates did not stay in the Ferry long;
after Antietam Lee backed down into the Valley. Mc-
Clellan chose the area for his bivouac. The great Army
of the Potomac filled the village and spread out over
the Heights, as it girded itself for yet another campaign with Richmond as its goal. This made for a
spectacle of grandeur, perhaps the last to be granted
the Ferry. Joseph Barry's *The Strange Story of Harpers Ferry*, a lively little volume now so precious the
Library of Congress locks it up in the Rare Book
Room, described the encampment:

> The whole peninsula formed by the Potomac and the
> Shenandoah . . . as well as the surrounding Heights, soon
> became dotted with tents and soon the two villages and
> the neighboring hills were aglow with hundreds of watch
> fires. From Camp Hill the spectacle was magnificent,
> especially at night. A hum of voices like that of an im-
> mense city or the hoarse murmur of the great deep arose
> from the valleys on either side and filled the air with a
> confusion of sounds. The bands of the various regiments
> frequently discoursed their martial strains, and nothing

that sight or sound could do to stir the imagination was wanted.

We have another distinguished visitor to the Ferry entering at this point. He did not share with Mr. Barry his awe at the gigantic encampment. President Lincoln, fearful that McClellan would again go into winter quarters without pressing for a decisive issue with Lee, arrived on October 1, 1862, to learn the general's plans. He arose early on the morning after his arrival and went for a walk just before dawn. As the morning fires began to twinkle and the brown dots of tents began to emerge from the mist Lincoln asked an officer, "Sir, what is this?"

"Why, Mr. President, this is the Army of the Potomac, of course."

"No," said Lincoln, and he was not being witty, "this is McClellan's bodyguard."

8

Appomattox. There is nothing left but the ruins of the old Works, just enough of them intact to be used for a small machine shop where battle-weary guns can be repaired.

We need an epitaph. It comes in a letter signed only "G.D." and addressed to a Mary Chapman of Frederick. It is written on that gimcrack paper hole-in-corner printers prepare for all wars, with a bunting border

and crossed American flags and all the rest of the hollowly patriotic ink-wasters. It is a simple lament, by a
boy who must have been very young.

Old Mrs. Powers poisoned three of our soldiers. They
were very hungry and went in to her house and she gave
them a chicken and a pie and two of them died right away
and the other lived a day and they have a guard on her
door now and won't let her sell anything to them. Allie
Powers hallooed "Hurrah for Jeff Davis!" and one of
the soldiers turned her across his knee and pulled up her
clothes and smacked her good. It serves her right, doesn't
it?

I tell you, Mary, the Ferry looks awful. You know I
was attached to it as much as anyone but I can truly say
I don't want to go back there to live until it is built up
again. The soldiers that are there are all strangers. The
houses look awful, the windows are all broken. Your
house is all shot up, the soldiers had been in it but there
is none there now. There was a great many pictures drawn
on the wall that the soldiers had been drawing . . .

epilogue

When a man is very old he is placed to sit in the sun, where he can be properly venerated. When a thing is very old it is put behind glass in a museum, for the moderns to marvel at. Our village is very old and quite quaint, so now they are going to preserve it.

The Interior Department has acquired the land— most of Shenandoah Street, the Harper house, and other portions of the town—to become our newest National Monument. The engine house, which was sent to the World's Fair in Chicago in 1894, used there as a stable, and at last brought back by Kate Field, the actress, will probably remain on the campus at Storer

College in Bolivar, the second institution of higher learning for Negroes established in the South.

The gun emplacements on the various heights will be restored, as they have been at Vicksburg. Gravel paths will lead here and there, to make it easy for the tourist. There will be souvenir shops and places to buy film and all the other appurtenances of a hallowed American spot.

And with all of this, it could be that the tradition of violence is dead and that the Ferry will begin to look happy, instead of haunted, as she has for so long.

to Martinsburg
& Wheeling

A MAP OF
HARPERS FERRY

which may be of some
assistance in locating
the important landmarks

1. Wall of Armory
2. Paymaster's Office
3. Engine House
4. Armory Gate
5. Water Tower
6. Galt House
7. Arsenal
8. Arsenal Gate
9. "Bloody Steps"
10. Harper House
11. Packing Horse Ford
    (about here)
12. B. & O. R. R.
13. Winchester & Potomac R. R.
14. Wager House and R. R. Station

to Charlestown,
Halltown &
Bolivar Heights

JEFFERSON'S
ROCK

VIRGINIUS
ISLAND

Hall's Works
on Southern End of
Virginius Is.